THE PROBLEM OF PAIN

Born in Ireland in 1898, c. s. LEWIS was educated at Malvern College for a year and then privately. He gained a triple First at Oxford and was a fellow and Tutor at Magdalen College 1925-54. In 1954 he became Professor of Mediaeval and Renaissance Literature at Cambridge. He was an outstanding and popular lecturer and had a lasting influence on his pupils.

C. S. Lewis was for many years an atheist, and described his conversion in *Surprised by Joy*: "In the Trinity Term of 1929 I gave in, and admitted that God was God . . . perhaps the most dejected and reluctant convert in England." It was this experience that helped him to understand not only apathy but active unwillingness to accept religion, and, as a Christian writer, gifted with an exceptionally brilliant and logical mind and a lucid, lively style, he was without peer. *The Problem of Pain*, *The Screwtape Letters*, *Mere Christianity*, *The Four Loves* and the posthumous *Letters to Malcolm, Chiefly on Prayer* are only a few of his best-selling works. He also wrote some delightful books for children and some science fiction, besides many works of literary criticism. His writings are known to millions of people all over the world in translation. He died on 22nd November 1963, at his home in Oxford.

by the same author

THE SCREWTAPE LETTERS
SURPRISED BY JOY
MERE CHRISTIANITY
MIRACLES
REFLECTIONS ON THE PSALMS
THE FOUR LOVES
SCREWTAPE PROPOSES A TOAST
and other pieces

C. S. LEWIS

The Problem of Pain

Collins
FOUNT PAPERBACKS

First published by Geoffrey Bles 1940
First issued in Fontana Books 1957
Reprinted in Fount Paperbacks January 1977
Eighteenth Impression October 1978

© C. S. Lewis 1940

Made and printed in Great Britain by
William Collins Sons & Co Ltd, Glasgow

To
The Inklings

The Son of God suffered unto the death, not that men might not suffer, but that their sufferings might be like His.

GEORGE MACDONALD,
Unspoken Sermons, First Series

PREFACE

When Mr. Ashley Sampson suggested to me the writing of this book, I asked leave to be allowed to write it anonymously, since, if I were to say what I really thought about pain, I should be forced to make statements of such apparent fortitude that they would become ridiculous if anyone knew who made them. Anonymity was rejected as inconsistent with the series; but Mr. Sampson pointed out that I could write a preface explaining that I did not live up to my own principles! This exhilarating programme I am now carrying out. Let me confess at once, in the words of good Walter Hilton, that throughout this book " I feel myself so far from true feeling of that I speak, that I can naught else but cry mercy and desire after it as I may ".[1] Yet for that very reason there is one criticism which cannot be brought against me. No one can say " He jests at scars who never felt a wound ", for I have never for one moment been in a state of mind to which even the imagination of serious pain was less than intolerable. If any man is safe from the danger of under-estimating this adversary, I am that man. I must add, too, that the only purpose of the book is to solve the intellectual problem raised by suffering; for the far higher task of teaching fortitude and patience I was never fool enough to suppose myself qualified, nor have I anything to offer

[1] *Scale of Perfection*, i, xvi.

my readers except my conviction that when pain is to be borne, a little courage helps more than much knowledge, a little human sympathy more than much courage, and the least tincture of the love of God more than all.

If any real theologian reads these pages he will very easily see that they are the work of a layman and an amateur. Except in the last two chapters, parts of which are admittedly speculative, I have believed myself to be re-stating ancient and orthodox doctrines. If any parts of the book are "original", in the sense of being novel or unorthodox, they are so against my will and as a result of my ignorance. I write, of course, as a layman of the Church of England : but I have tried to assume nothing that is not professed by all baptised and communicating Christians.

As this is not a work of erudition I have taken little pains to trace ideas or quotations to their sources when they were not easily recoverable. Any theologian will see easily enough what, and how little, I have read.

C. S. LEWIS.

Magdalen College, Oxford.

1940.

CONTENTS

I. INTRODUCTORY

I wonder at the hardihood with which such persons undertake to talk about God. In a treatise addressed to infidels they begin with a chapter proving the existence of God from the works of Nature . . . this only gives their readers grounds for thinking that the proofs of our religion are very weak. . . . It is a remarkable fact that no canonical writer has ever used Nature to prove God.

PASCAL. *Pensées*, IV, 242, 243.

NOT many years ago when I was an atheist, if anyone had asked me, " Why do you not believe in God ? " my reply would have run something like this : " Look at the universe we live in. By far the greatest part of it consists of empty space, completely dark and unimaginably cold. The bodies which move in this space are so few and so small in comparison with the space itself that even if every one of them were known to be crowded as full as it could hold with perfectly happy creatures, it would still be difficult to believe that life and happiness were more than a bye-product to the power that made the universe. As it is, however, the scientists think it likely that very few of the suns of space—perhaps none of them except our own—have any planets ; and in our own system it is improbable that any planet except the Earth sustains life. And Earth herself existed without life for millions of years and may exist for millions more when life has left her. And what is it like while it lasts ? It is so arranged that all the forms of it can live only by preying upon one another. In the lower forms this process entails only death, but in the higher there appears a new quality called consciousness which enables it to be attended with pain. The creatures cause pain by being born, and live by inflicting pain, and in pain they mostly die. In the most complex of all the creatures, Man, yet another quality appears, which we call reason, whereby he is enabled to foresee his own pain which henceforth is preceded with acute mental suffering, and to foresee his own death while keenly desiring permanence. It also enables men by a hundred ingenious contrivances to inflict a great deal more pain than they otherwise could have done on one another and on the irrational creatures. This power they have exploited to the full. Their history is largely a record of crime, war, disease, and terror, with just sufficient happiness interposed to give them, while it lasts, an agonised apprehension of losing it, and, when it is lost, the poignant misery of remembering. Every now and then they improve their condition a little and what we call a civilisation appears. But all civilisations pass away and, even while they remain, inflict peculiar sufferings of their own probably sufficient to outweigh what alleviations they may have brought to the normal pains of man. That our own civilisation has done so, no one will dispute; that it will pass away like all its predecessors is surely probable. Even if it should not, what then ? The race is doomed. Every race that comes into being in any part of the universe is doomed; for the universe, they tell us, is running down, and will sometime be a uniform infinity of homogeneous matter at a low temperature. All stories will come to nothing : all life will turn out in the end to have been a transitory and senseless contortion upon the idiotic face of infinite matter. If you ask me to believe that this is the work of a benevolent and omnipotent spirit, I reply that all the evidence points in the opposite direction. Either there is no spirit behind the universe, or else a spirit indifferent to good and evil, or else an evil spirit."

There was one question which I never dreamed of raising. I never noticed that the very strength and facility of the pessimists' case at once poses us a problem. If the universe is so bad, or even half so bad, how on earth did human beings ever come to attribute it to the activity of a wise and good Creator ? Men are fools, perhaps ; but hardly so foolish as that. The direct inference from black to white, from evil flower to virtuous root, from senseless work to a workman infinitely wise, staggers belief. The spectacle of the universe as revealed by experience can never have been the ground of religion : it must always have been something in spite of which religion, acquired from a different source, was held.

It would be an error to reply that our ancestors were ignorant and therefore entertained pleasing illusions about nature which the progress of science has since dispelled. For centuries, during which all men believed, the nightmare size and emptiness of the universe was already known. You will read in some books that the men of the Middle Ages thought the Earth flat and the stars near, but that is a lie. Ptolemy had told them that the Earth was a mathematical point without size in relation to the distance of the fixed stars—a distance which one mediæval popular text estimates as a hundred and seventeen million miles. And in times yet earlier, even from the beginnings, men must have got the same sense of hostile immensity from a more obvious source. To prehistoric man the neighbouring forest must have been infinite enough, and the utterly alien and infest which we have to fetch from the thought of cosmic rays and cooling suns, came snuffing and howling nightly to his very doors. Certainly at all periods the pain and waste of human life was equally obvious. Our own religion begins among the Jews, a people squeezed between great warlike empires, continually defeated and led captive, familiar as Poland or Armenia with the tragic story of the conquered. It is mere nonsense to put pain among the discoveries of science. Lay down this book and reflect for five minutes on the fact that all the great religions were first preached, and long practised, in a world without chloroform.

At all times, then, an inference from the course of events in this world to the goodness and wisdom of the Creator would have been equally preposterous; and it was never made.[1] Religion has a different origin. In what follows it must be understood that I am not *primarily* arguing the truth of Christianity but describing its origin—a task, in my view, necessary if we are to put the problem of pain in its right setting.

In all developed religion we find three strands or elements, and in Christianity one more. The first of these is what Professor Otto calls the experience of the *Numinous*. Those who have not met this term

---

[1] *I.e.*, never made at the beginnings of a religion. *After* belief in God has been accepted, " theodicies " explaining, or explaining away, the miseries of life, will naturally appear often enough.

may be introduced to it by the following device. Suppose you were told there was a tiger in the next room : you would know that you were in danger and would probably feel fear. But if you were told " There is a ghost in the next room ", and believed it, you would feel, indeed, what is often called fear, but of a different kind. It would not be based on the knowledge of danger, for no one is primarily afraid of what a ghost may do to him, but of the mere fact that it is a ghost. It is " uncanny " rather than dangerous, and the special kind of fear it excites may be called Dread. With the Uncanny one has reached the fringes of the Numinous. Now suppose that you were told simply " There is a mighty spirit in the room ", and believed it. Your feelings would then be even less like the mere fear of danger : but the disturbance would be profound. You would feel wonder and a certain shrinking—a sense of inadequacy to cope with such a visitant and of prostration before it—an emotion which might be expressed in Shakespeare's words " Under it my genius is rebuked ". This feeling may be described as awe, and the object which excites it as the *Numinous*.

Now nothing is more certain than that man, from a very early period, began to believe that the universe was haunted by spirits. Professor Otto perhaps assumes too easily that from the very first such spirits were regarded with numinous awe. This is impossible to prove for the very good reason that utterances expressing awe of the Numinous and utterances expressing mere fear of danger may use identical language—as we can still say that we are " afraid " of a ghost or " afraid " of a rise in prices.

It is therefore theoretically possible that there was a time when men regarded these spirits simply as dangerous and felt towards them just as they felt towards tigers. What is certain is that now, at any rate, the numinous experience exists and that if we start from ourselves we can trace it a long way back.

A modern example may be found (if we are not too proud to seek it there) in *The Wind in the Willows* where Rat and Mole approach Pan on the island.

" ' Rat,' he found breath to whisper, shaking, ' Are you afraid ? ' ' Afraid ? ' murmured the Rat, his eyes shining with unutterable love. ' Afraid ? of Him ? O, never, never. And yet—and yet—O Mole, I am afraid.' "

Going back about a century we find copious examples in Wordsworth—perhaps the finest being that passage in the first book of the *Prelude* where he describes his experience while rowing on the lake in the stolen boat. Going back further we get a very pure and strong example in Malory,[1] when Galahad " began to tremble right hard when the deadly (= mortal) flesh began to behold the spiritual things ". At the beginning of our era it finds expression in the Apocalypse where the writer fell at the feet of the risen Christ " as one dead ". In Pagan literature we find Ovid's picture of the dark grove on the Aventine of which you would say at a glance *numen inest*[2]—the place is haunted, or there is a Presence here ; and Virgil gives us the palace of Latinus " awful (*horrendum*) with woods and sanctity

---

[1] XVII, xxii.
[2] *Fasti*, III, 296.

(*religione*) of elder days ".[1]   A Greek fragment attributed, but improbably, to Æschylus, tells us of earth, sea, and mountain shaking beneath the " dread eye of their Master ".[2]   And far further back Ezekiel tells us of the " rings " in his Theophany that " they were so high that they were dreadful " [3] : and Jacob, rising from sleep, says " How dreadful is this place ! " [4]

We do not know how far back in human history this feeling goes. The earliest men almost certainly believed in things which would excite the feeling in us if *we* believed in them, and it seems therefore probable that numinous awe is as old as humanity itself. But our main concern is not with its dates. The important thing is that somehow or other it has come into existence, and is widespread, and does not disappear from the mind with the growth of knowledge and civilisation.

Now this awe is not the result of an inference from the visible universe. There is no possibility of arguing from mere danger to the uncanny, still less to the fully Numinous. You may say that it seems to you very natural that early man, being surrounded by real dangers, and therefore frightened, should invent the uncanny and the Numinous. In a sense it is, but let us understand what we mean. You feel it to be natural because, sharing human nature with your remote ancestors, you can imagine yourself reacting to perilous solitudes in the same way ; and this reaction is indeed " natural " in the sense of being

[1] *Aen.* VII, 172.
[2] Fragm. 464. Sidgwick's edition.
[3] Ezek. i, 18.
[4] Gen. xxviii, 17.

in accord with human nature. But it is not in the
least "natural" in the sense that the idea of the
uncanny or the Numinous is already contained in the
idea of the dangerous, or that any perception of
danger or any dislike of the wounds and death which
it may entail could give the slightest conception of
ghostly dread or numinous awe to an intelligence
which did not already understand them. When man
passes from physical fear to dread and awe, he makes
a sheer jump, and apprehends something which could
never be *given*, as danger is, by the physical facts and
logical deductions from them. Most attempts to
explain the Numinous presuppose the thing to be
explained—as when anthropologists derive it from
fear of the dead, without explaining why dead men
(assuredly the least dangerous kind of men) should
have attracted this peculiar feeling. Against all such
attempts we must insist that dread and awe are in a
different dimension from fear. They are in the
nature of an interpretation man gives to the universe,
or an impression he gets from it; and just as no
enumeration of the physical qualities of a beautiful
object could ever include its beauty, or give the
faintest hint of what we mean by beauty to a creature
without æsthetic experience, so no factual description
of any human environment could include the uncanny
and the Numinous or even hint at them. There seem,
in fact, to be only two views we can hold about awe.
Either it is a mere twist in the human mind, corresponding to nothing objective and serving no biological
function, yet showing no tendency to disappear from
that mind at its fullest development in poet,
philosopher, or saint : or else it is a direct experience

of the really supernatural, to which the name
Revelation might properly be given.

The Numinous is not the same as the morally good,
and a man overwhelmed with awe is likely, if left to
himself, to think the numinous object " beyond good
and evil." This brings us to the second strand or
element in religion. All the human beings that
history has heard of acknowledge some kind of
morality ; that is, they feel towards certain proposed
actions the experiences expressed by the words " I
ought " or " I ought not ". These experiences
resemble awe in one respect, namely that they cannot
be logically deduced from the environment and
physical experiences of the man who undergoes them.
You can shuffle " I want " and " I am forced " and
" I shall be well advised " and " I dare not " as long
as you please without getting out of them the slightest
hint of " ought " and " ought not ". And, once again,
attempts to resolve the moral experience into something else always presuppose the very thing they are
trying to explain—as when a famous psycho-analyst
deduces it from prehistoric parricide. If the parricide
produced a sense of guilt, that was because men felt
that they ought not to have committed it : if they did
not so feel, it could produce no sense of guilt.
Morality, like numinous awe, is a jump ; in it, man
goes beyond anything that can be " given " in the
facts of experience. And it has one characteristic too
remarkable to be ignored. The moralities accepted
among men may differ—though not, at bottom, so
widely as is often claimed—but they all agree in
prescribing a behaviour which their adherents fail to
practise. All men alike stand condemned, not by

alien codes of ethics, but by their own, and all men therefore are conscious of guilt. The second element in religion is the consciousness not merely of a moral law, but of a moral law at once approved and disobeyed. This consciousness is neither a logical, nor an illogical, inference from the facts of experience; if we did not bring it to our experience we could not find it there. It is either inexplicable illusion, or else revelation.

The moral experience and the numinous experience are so far from being the same that they may exist for quite long periods without establishing a mutual contact. In many forms of Paganism the worship of the gods and the ethical discussions of the philosophers have very little to do with each other. The third stage in religious development arises when men identify them—when the Numinous Power to which they feel awe is made the guardian of the morality to which they feel obligation. Once again, this may seem to you very "natural". What can be more natural than for a savage haunted at once by awe and by guilt to think that the power which awes him is also the authority which condemns his guilt? And it is, indeed, natural to humanity. But it is not in the least obvious. The actual behaviour of that universe which the Numinous haunts bears no resemblance to the behaviour which morality demands of us. The one seems wasteful, ruthless, and unjust; the other enjoins upon us the opposite qualities. Nor can the identification of the two be explained as a wish-fulfilment, for it fulfils no one's wishes. We desire nothing less than to see that Law whose naked authority is already unsupportable armed with the incalculable claims of the Numinous. Of all the jumps that humanity takes in its religious history this is certainly the most surprising. It is not unnatural that many sections of the human race refused it; non-moral religion, and non-religious morality, existed and still exist. Perhaps only a single people, as a people, took the new step with perfect decision—I mean the Jews: but great individuals in all times and places have taken it also, and only those who take it are safe from the obscenities and barbarities of unmoralised worship or the cold, sad self-righteousness of sheer moralism. Judged by its fruits, this step is a step towards increased health. And though logic does not compel us to take it, it is very hard to resist—even on Paganism and Pantheism morality is always breaking in, and even Stoicism finds itself willy-nilly bowing the knee to God. Once more, it may be madness—a madness congenital to man and oddly fortunate in its results—or it may be revelation. And if revelation, then it is most really and truly in Abraham that all peoples shall be blessed, for it was the Jews who fully and unambiguously identified the awful Presence haunting black mountain-tops and thunderclouds with " the *righteous* Lord " who " loveth righteousness ".[1]

The fourth strand or element is a historical event. There was a man born among these Jews who claimed to be, or to be the son of, or to be " one with ", the Something which is at once the awful haunter of nature and the giver of the moral law. The claim is so shocking—a paradox, and even a horror, which we may easily be lulled into taking too lightly—that only two views of this man are possible. Either he

[1] Ps. xi, 8.

was a raving lunatic of an unusually abominable type, or else He was, and is, precisely what He said. There is no middle way. If the records make the first hypothesis unacceptable, you must submit to the second. And if you do that, all else that is claimed by Christians becomes credible—that this Man, having been killed, was yet alive, and that His death, in some manner incomprehensible to human thought, has effected a real change in our relations to the "awful" and "righteous" Lord, and a change in our favour.

To ask whether the universe as we see it looks more like the work of a wise and good Creator or the work of chance, indifference, or malevolence, is to omit from the outset all the relevant factors in the religious problem. Christianity is not the conclusion of a philosophical debate on the origins of the universe : it is a catastrophic historical event following on the long spiritual preparation of humanity which I have described. It is not a system into which we have to fit the awkward fact of pain : it is itself one of the awkward facts which have to be fitted into any system we make. In a sense, it creates, rather than solves, the problem of pain, for pain would be no problem unless, side by side with our daily experience of this painful world, we had received what we think a good assurance that ultimate reality is righteous and loving.

Why this assurance seems to me good, I have more or less indicated. It does not amount to logical compulsion. At every stage of religious development man may rebel, if not without violence to his own nature, yet without absurdity. He can close his spiritual eyes against the Numinous, if he is prepared to part company with half the great poets and prophets of his race, with his own childhood, with the richness and depth of uninhibited experience. He can regard the moral law as an illusion, and so cut himself off from the common ground of humanity. He can refuse to identify the Numinous with the righteous, and remain a barbarian, worshipping sexuality, or the dead, or the life-force, or the future. But the cost is heavy. And when we come to the last step of all, the historical Incarnation, the assurance is strongest of all. The story is strangely like many myths which have haunted religion from the first, and yet it is not like them. It is not transparent to the reason: we could not have invented it ourselves. It has not the suspicious *a priori* lucidity of Pantheism or of Newtonian physics. It has the seemingly arbitrary and idiosyncratic character which modern science is slowly teaching us to put up with in this wilful universe, where energy is made up in little parcels of a quantity no one could predict, where speed is not unlimited, where irreversible entropy gives time a real direction and the cosmos, no longer static or cyclic, moves like a drama from a real beginning to a real end. If any message from the core of reality ever were to reach us, we should expect to find in it just that unexpectedness, that wilful, dramatic anfractuosity which we find in the Christian faith. It has the master touch—the rough, male taste of reality, not made by us, or, indeed, for us, but hitting us in the face.

If, on such grounds, or on better ones, we follow the course on which humanity has been led, and become Christians, we then have the " problem " of pain.

II. DIVINE OMNIPOTENCE

Nothing which implies contradiction falls under the omnipotence of God.

THOMAS AQUINAS. *Summ. Theol.*, Iᵃ Q XXV, Art. 4.

"IF God were good, He would wish to make His creatures perfectly happy, and if God were almighty He would be able to do what He wished. But the creatures are not happy. Therefore God lacks either goodness, or power, or both." This is the problem of pain, in its simplest form. The possibility of answering it depends on showing that the terms "good" and "almighty", and perhaps also the term "happy" are equivocal : for it must be admitted from the outset that if the popular meanings attached to these words are the best, or the only possible, meanings, then the argument is unanswerable. In this chapter I shall make some comments on the idea of Omnipotence, and, in the following, some on the idea of Goodness.

Omnipotence means "power to do all, or everything".[1] And we are told in Scripture that "with God all things are possible". It is common enough, in argument with an unbeliever, to be told that God, if He existed and were good, would do this or that ; and then, if we point out that the proposed action is impossible, to be met with the retort, "But I thought

---

[1] The original meaning in Latin may have been "power *over* or *in* all". I give what I take to be current sense.

God was supposed to be able to do anything ". This raises the whole question of impossibility.

In ordinary usage the word *impossible* generally implies a suppressed clause beginning with the word *unless*. Thus it is impossible for me to see the street from where I sit writing at this moment; that is, it is impossible to see the street *unless* I go up to the top floor where I shall be high enough to overlook the intervening building. If I had broken my leg I should say " But it is impossible to go up to the top floor "— meaning, however, that it is impossible *unless* some friends turn up who will carry me. Now let us advance to a different plane of impossibility, by saying " It is, at any rate, impossible to see the street *so long as* I remain where I am and the intervening building remains where it is." Someone might add " unless the nature of space, or of vision, were different from what it is ". I do not know what the best philosophers and scientists would say to this, but I should have to reply " I don't know whether space and vision *could possibly* have been of such a nature as you suggest ". Now it is clear that the words *could possibly* here refer to some absolute kind of possibility or impossibility which is different from the relative possibilities and impossibilities we have been considering. I cannot say whether seeing round corners is, in this new sense, possible or not, because I do not know whether it is self-contradictory or not. But I know very well that if it is self-contradictory it is absolutely impossible. The absolutely impossible may also be called the intrinsically impossible because it carries its impossibility within itself, instead of borrowing it from other impossibilities which in their turn depend upon others. It has no *unless* clause attached to it. It is impossible under all conditions and in all worlds and for all agents.

"All agents" here includes God Himself. His Omnipotence means power to do all that is intrinsically possible, not to do the intrinsically impossible. You may attribute miracles to Him, but not nonsense. This is no limit to His power. If you choose to say "God can give a creature free-will and at the same time withhold free-will from it," you have not succeeded in saying *anything* about God : meaningless combinations of words do not suddenly acquire meaning simply because we prefix to them the two other words "God can". It remains true that all *things* are possible with God : the intrinsic impossibilities are not things but nonentities. It is no more possible for God than for the weakest of His creatures to carry out both of two mutually exclusive alternatives ; not because His power meets an obstacle, but because nonsense remains nonsense even when we talk it about God.

It should, however, be remembered that human reasoners often make mistakes, either by arguing from false data or by inadvertence in the argument itself. We may thus come to think things possible which are really impossible, and *vice versâ*.[1] We ought, therefore, to use great caution in defining those intrinsic impossibilities which even Omnipotence cannot perform. What follows is to be regarded less as an assertion of what they are than a sample of what they might be like.

[1] *E.g.*, every good conjuring trick does something which to the audience with their *data* and their power of reasoning, seems self-contradictory.

The inexorable "laws of Nature" which operate in defiance of human suffering or desert, which are not turned aside by prayer, seem, at first sight to furnish a strong argument against the goodness and power of God. I am going to submit that not even Omnipotence could create a society of free souls without at the same time creating a relatively independent and "inexorable" Nature.

There is no reason to suppose that self-consciousness, the recognition of a creature by itself as a "self", can exist except in contrast with an "other", a something which is not the self. It is against an environment, and preferably a social environment, an environment of other selves, that the awareness of Myself stands out. This would raise a difficulty about the consciousness of God if we were mere theists: being Christians, we learn from the doctrine of the Blessed Trinity that something analogous to "society" exists within the Divine being from all eternity—that God is Love, not merely in the sense of being the Platonic form of love, but because, within Him, the concrete reciprocities of love exist before all worlds and are thence derived to the creatures.

Again, the freedom of a creature must mean freedom to choose: and choice implies the existence of things to choose between. A creature with no environment would have no choices to make: so that freedom, like self-consciousness (if they are not, indeed, the same thing) again demands the presence to the self of something other than the self.

The minimum condition of self-consciousness and freedom, then, would be that the creature should apprehend God and, therefore, itself as distinct from God. It is possible that such creatures exist, aware of God and themselves, but of no fellow-creatures. If so, their freedom is simply that of making a single naked choice—of loving God more than the self or the self more than God. But a life so reduced to essentials is not imaginable to us. As soon as we attempt to introduce the mutual knowledge of fellow-creatures we run up against the necessity of " Nature ".

People often talk as if nothing were easier than for two naked minds to " meet " or become aware of each other. But I see no possibility of their doing so except in a common medium which forms their " external world " or environment. Even our vague attempt to imagine such a meeting between dis-embodied spirits usually slips in surreptitiously the idea of, at least, a common space and common time, to give the co- in co-existence a meaning : and space and time are already an environment. But more than this is required. If your thoughts and passions were directly present to me, like my own, without any mark of externality or otherness, how should I distinguish them from mine ? And what thoughts or passions could we begin to have without objects to think and feel about ? Nay, could I even begin to have the conception of " external " and " other " unless I had experience of an " external world " ? You may reply, as a Christian, that God (and Satan) do, in fact, affect my consciousness in this direct way without signs of " externality ". Yes : and the result is that most people remain ignorant of the existence of both. We may therefore suppose that if human souls affected one another directly and immaterially, it would be a rare triumph of faith and insight for any one of them to believe in the existence of the others. It would be harder for me to know my neighbour under such conditions than it now is for me to know God : for in recognising the impact of God upon me I am now helped by things that reach me through the external world, such as the tradition of the Church, Holy Scripture, and the conversation of religious friends. What we need for human society is exactly what we have—a neutral something, neither you nor I, which we can both manipulate so as to make signs to each other. I can talk to you because we can both set up sound-waves in the common air between us. Matter, which keeps souls apart, also brings them together. It enables each of us to have an " outside " as well as an " inside ", so that what are acts of will and thought for you are noises and glances for me ; you are enabled not only to *be*, but to *appear* : and hence I have the pleasure of making your acquaintance.

Society, then, implies a common field or " world " in which its members meet. If there is an angelic society, as Christians have usually believed, then the angels also must have such a world or field ; something which is to them as " matter " (in the modern, not the scholastic, sense) is to us.

But if matter is to serve as a neutral field it must have a fixed nature of its own. If a " world " or material system had only a single inhabitant it might conform at every moment to his wishes—" trees for his sake would crowd into a shade ". But if you were introduced into a world which thus varied at my every whim, you would be quite unable to act in it and would thus lose the exercise of your free will.

Nor is it clear that you could make your presence
known to me—all the matter by which you attempted
to make signs to me being already in my control and
therefore not capable of being manipulated by you.

Again, if matter has a fixed nature and obeys
constant laws, not all states of matter will be equally
agreeable to the wishes of a given soul, nor all equally
beneficial for that particular aggregate of matter
which he calls his body. If fire comforts that body
at a certain distance, it will destroy it when the
distance is reduced. Hence, even in a perfect world,
the necessity for those danger signals which the
pain-fibres in our nerves are apparently designed to
transmit. Does this mean an inevitable element of
evil (in the form of pain) in any possible world? I
think not: for while it may be true that the least sin
is an incalculable evil, the evil of pain depends on
degree, and pains below a certain intensity are not
feared or resented at all. No one minds the process
" warm—beautifully hot—too hot—it stings " which
warns him to withdraw his hand from exposure to the
fire : and, if I may trust my own feeling, a slight
aching in the legs as we climb into bed after a good
day's walking is, in fact, pleasurable.

Yet again, if the fixed nature of matter prevents it
from being always, and in all its dispositions, equally
agreeable even to a single soul, much less is it possible
for the matter of the universe at any moment to be
distributed so that it is equally convenient and
pleasurable to each member of a society. If a man
travelling in one direction is having a journey down
hill, a man going in the opposite direction must be
going up hill. If even a pebble lies where I want it

to lie, it cannot, except by a coincidence, be where you want it to lie. And this is very far from being an evil: on the contrary, it furnishes occasion for all those acts of courtesy, respect, and unselfishness by which love and good humour and modesty express themselves. But it certainly leaves the way open to a great evil, that of competition and hostility. And if souls are free, they cannot be prevented from dealing with the problem by competition instead of by courtesy. And once they have advanced to actual hostility, they can then exploit the fixed nature of matter to hurt one another. The permanent nature of wood which enables us to use it as a beam also enables us to use it for hitting our neighbour on the head. The permanent nature of matter in general means that when human beings fight, the victory ordinarily goes to those who have superior weapons, skill, and numbers, even if their cause is unjust.

We can, perhaps, conceive of a world in which God corrected the results of this abuse of free-will by His creatures at every moment: so that a wooden beam became soft as grass when it was used as a weapon, and the air refused to obey me if I attempted to set up in it the sound waves that carry lies or insults. But such a world would be one in which wrong actions were impossible, and in which, therefore, freedom of the will would be void; nay, if the principle were carried out to its logical conclusion, evil thoughts would be impossible, for the cerebral matter which we use in thinking would refuse its task when we attempted to frame them. All matter in the neighbourhood of a wicked man would be liable to undergo unpredictable alterations. That God can and does, on occasions, modify the behaviour of matter and produce what we call miracles, is part of the Christian faith; but the very conception of a common, and therefore, stable, world, demands that these occasions should be extremely rare. In a game of chess you can make certain arbitrary concessions to your opponent, which stand to the ordinary rules of the game as miracles stand to the laws of nature. You can deprive yourself of a castle, or allow the other man sometimes to take back a move made inadvertently. But if you conceded everything that at any moment happened to suit him—if all his moves were revocable and if all your pieces disappeared whenever their position on the board was not to his liking— then you could not have a game at all. So it is with the life of souls in a world : fixed laws, consequences unfolding by causal necessity, the whole natural order, are at once the limits within which their common life is confined and also the sole condition under which any such life is possible. Try to exclude the possibility of suffering which the order of nature and the existence of free-wills involve, and you find that you have excluded life itself.

As I said before, this account of the intrinsic necessities of a world is meant merely as a specimen of what they might be. What they really are, only Omniscience has the data and the wisdom to see : but they are not likely to be *less* complicated than I have suggested. Needless to say, "complicated" here refers solely to the human understanding of them ; we are not to think of God arguing, as we do, from an end (co-existence of free spirits) to the conditions involved in it, but rather of a single, utterly self-consistent act of creation which to us appears, at first sight, as the creation of many independent things, and then, as the creation of things mutually necessary. Even we can rise a little beyond the conception of mutual necessities as I have outlined it—can reduce matter as that which separates souls and matter as that which brings them together under the single concept of Plurality, whereof " separation " and " togetherness " are only two aspects. With every advance in our thought the unity of the creative act, and the impossibility of tinkering with the creation as though this or that element of it could have been removed, will become more apparent. Perhaps this is not the " best of all possible " universes, but the only possible one. Possible worlds can mean only " worlds that God could have made, but didn't ". The idea of that which God " could have " done involves a too anthropomorphic conception of God's freedom. Whatever human freedom means, Divine freedom cannot mean indeterminacy between alternatives and choice of one of them. Perfect goodness can never debate about the end to be attained, and perfect wisdom cannot debate about the means most suited to achieve it. The freedom of God consists in the fact that no cause other than Himself produces His acts and no external obstacle impedes them—that His own goodness is the root from which they all grow and His own omnipotence the air in which they all flower.

And that brings us to our next subject—the Divine goodness. Nothing so far has been said of this, and no answer attempted to the objection that if the universe must, from the outset, admit the possibility

P.P.

B

of suffering, then absolute goodness would have left the universe uncreated. And I must warn the reader that I shall not attempt to prove that to create was better than not to create: I am aware of no human scales in which such a portentous question can be weighed. Some comparison between one state of being and another can be made, but the attempt to compare being and not being ends in mere words. " It would be better for me not to exist "—in what sense " for me " ? How should I, if I did not exist, profit by not existing ? Our design is a less formidable one : it is only to discover how, perceiving a suffering world, and being assured, on quite different grounds, that God is good, we are to conceive that goodness and that suffering without contradiction.

III. DIVINE GOODNESS

Love can forbear, and Love can forgive . . . but Love can
never be reconciled to an unlovely object. . . . He can never
therefore be reconciled to your sin, because sin itself is incapable
of being altered ; but He may be reconciled to your person,
because that may be restored.

TRAHERNE. *Centuries of Meditation*, II, 30.

ANY consideration of the goodness of God at once
threatens us with the following dilemma.

On the one hand, if God is wiser than we His
judgement must differ from ours on many things, and
not least on good and evil. What seems to us good
may therefore not be good in His eyes, and what
seems to us evil may not be evil.

On the other hand, if God's moral judgement
differs from ours so that our " black " may be His
" white ", we can mean nothing by calling Him good ;
for to say " God is good," while asserting that His
goodness is wholly other than ours, is really only to
say " God is we know not what ". And an utterly
unknown quality in God cannot give us moral
grounds for loving or obeying Him. If He is not (in
our sense) " good " we shall obey, if at all, only
through fear—and should be equally ready to obey
an omnipotent Fiend. The doctrine of Total
Depravity—when the consequence is drawn that,
since we are totally depraved, our idea of good is
worth simply nothing—may thus turn Christianity
into a form of devil-worship.

The escape from this dilemma depends on observing what happens, in human relations, when the man of inferior moral standards enters the society of those who are better and wiser than he and gradually learns to accept *their* standards—a process which, as it happens, I can describe fairly accurately, since I have undergone it. When I came first to the University I was as nearly without a moral conscience as a boy could be. Some faint distaste for cruelty and for meanness about money was my utmost reach—of chastity, truthfulness, and self sacrifice I thought as a baboon thinks of classical music. By the mercy of God I fell among a set of young men (none of them, by the way, Christians) who were sufficiently close to me in intellect and imagination to secure immediate intimacy, but who knew, and tried to obey, the moral law. Thus their judgement of good and evil was very different from mine. Now what happens in such a case is not in the least like being asked to treat as " white " what was hitherto called black. The new moral judgements never enter the mind as mere reversals (though they do reverse them) of previous judgements but " as lords that are certainly expected ". You can have no doubt in which direction you are moving : they are more like good than the little shreds of good you already had, but are, in a sense, continuous with them. But the great test is that the recognition of the new standards is accompanied with the sense of shame and guilt : one is conscious of having blundered into society that one is unfit for. It is in the light of such experiences that we must consider the goodness of God. Beyond all doubt, His idea of " goodness " differs from ours ; but you need have no fear that, as you approach it, you will be asked simply to reverse your moral standards. When the relevant difference between the Divine ethics and your own appears to you, you will not, in fact, be in any doubt that the change demanded of you is in the direction you already call " better ". The Divine " goodness " differs from ours, but it is not sheerly different : it differs from ours not as white from black but as a perfect circle from a child's first attempt to draw a wheel. But when the child has learned to draw, it will know that the circle it then makes is what it was trying to make from the very beginning.

This doctrine is presupposed in Scripture. Christ calls men to repent—a call which would be meaningless if God's standard were sheerly different from that which they already knew and failed to practise. He appeals to our existing moral judgement—" Why even of yourselves judge ye not what is right ? " [1] God in the Old Testament expostulates with men on the basis of their own conceptions of gratitude, fidelity, and fair play : and puts Himself, as it were, at the bar before His own creatures—" What iniquity have your fathers found in me, that they are gone far from me ? " [2]

After these preliminaries it will, I hope, be safe to suggest that some conceptions of the Divine goodness which tend to dominate our thought, though seldom expressed in so many words, are open to criticism.

By the goodness of God we mean nowadays almost exclusively His lovingness; and in this we may be

[1] Luke xii, 57.
[2] Jer. ii, 5.

right. And by Love, in this context, most of us mean
kindness—the desire to see others than the self
happy ; not happy in this way or in that, but just
happy. What would really satisfy us would be a
God who said of anything we happened to like doing,
" What does it matter so long as they are contented ? "
We want, in fact, not so much a Father in Heaven as
a grandfather in heaven—a senile benevolence who,
as they say, " liked to see young people enjoying
themselves " and whose plan for the universe was
simply that it might be truly said at the end of each
day, " a good time was had by all ". Not many
people, I admit, would formulate a theology in
precisely those terms : but a conception not very
different lurks at the back of many minds. I do not
claim to be an exception : I should very much like
to live in a universe which was governed on such
lines. But since it is abundantly clear that I don't,
and since I have reason to believe, nevertheless, that
God is Love, I conclude that my conception of love
needs correction.

I might, indeed, have learned, even from the poets,
that Love is something more stern and splendid than
mere kindness : that even the love between the sexes
is, as in Dante, " a lord of terrible aspect ". There is
kindness in Love : but Love and kindness are not
coterminous, and when kindness (in the sense given
above) is separated from the other elements of Love,
it involves a certain fundamental indifference to its
object, and even something like contempt of it.
Kindness consents very readily to the removal of its
object—we have all met people whose kindness to
animals is constantly leading them to kill animals lest

they should suffer. Kindness, merely as such, cares
not whether its object becomes good or bad, provided
only that it escapes suffering. As Scripture points
out, it is bastards who are spoiled : the legitimate
sons, who are to carry on the family tradition, are
punished.[1] It is for people whom we care nothing
about that we demand happiness on any terms : with
our friends, our lovers, our children, we are exacting
and would rather see them suffer much than be happy
in contemptible and estranging modes. If God is
Love, He is, by definition, something more than mere
kindness. And it appears, from all the records, that
though He has often rebuked us and condemned us,
He has never regarded us with contempt. He has
paid us the intolerable compliment of loving us, in the
deepest, most tragic, most inexorable sense.

The relation between Creator and creature is, of
course, unique, and cannot be paralleled by any
relations between one creature and another. God is
both further from us, and nearer to us, than any other
being. He is further from us because the sheer
difference between that which has Its principle of
being in Itself and that to which being is communicated, is one compared with which the difference
between an archangel and a worm is quite insignificant.
He makes, we are made : He is original, we derivative.
But at the same time, and for the same reason, the
intimacy between God and even the meanest creature
is closer than any that creatures can attain with one
another. Our life is, at every moment, supplied by
Him : our tiny, miraculous power of free will only
operates on bodies which His continual energy keeps

[1] Heb. xii, 8.

in existence—our very power to think is His power
communicated to us. Such a unique relation can be
apprehended only by analogies : from the various
types of love known among creatures we reach an
inadequate, but useful, conception of God's love for
man.

The lowest type, and one which is "love" at all
only by an extension of the word, is that which an
artist feels for an artefact. God's relation to man is
pictured thus in Jeremiah's vision of the potter and
the clay,[1] or when St. Peter speaks of the whole
Church as a building on which God is at work, and
of the individual members as stones.[2] The limitation
of such an analogy is, of course, that in the symbol
the patient is not sentient, and that certain questions
of justice and mercy which arise when the "stones"
are really "living" therefore remain unrepresented.
But it is an important analogy so far as it goes. We
are, not metaphorically but in very truth, a Divine
work of art, something that God is making, and
therefore something with which He will not be
satisfied until it has a certain character. Here again
we come up against what I have called the "intolerable
compliment". Over a sketch made idly to amuse a
child, an artist may not take much trouble : he may
be content to let it go even though it is not exactly
as he meant it to be. But over the great picture of his
life—the work which he loves, though in a different
fashion, as intensely as a man loves a woman or a
mother a child—he will take endless trouble—and
would, doubtless, thereby *give* endless trouble to the

picture if it were sentient. One can imagine a
sentient picture, after being rubbed and scraped and
re-commenced for the tenth time, wishing that it
were only a thumb-nail sketch whose making was over
in a minute. In the same way, it is natural for us
to wish that God had designed for us a less glorious
and less arduous destiny; but then we are wishing
not for more love but for less.

Another type is the love of a man for a beast—a
relation constantly used in Scripture to symbolise the
relation between God and men; " we are his people
and the sheep of his pasture ". This is in some ways
a better analogy than the preceding, because the
inferior party is sentient, and yet unmistakably
inferior : but it is less good in so far as man has not
made the beast and does not fully understand it. Its
great merit lies in the fact that the association of (say)
man and dog is primarily for the man's sake : he tames
the dog primarily that he may love it, not that it may
love him, and that it may serve him, not that he may
serve it. Yet at the same time, the dog's interests are
not sacrificed to the man's. The one end (that he
may love it) cannot be fully attained unless it also,
in its fashion, loves him, nor can it serve him unless
he, in a different fashion, serves it. Now just because
the dog is by human standards one of the " best " of
irrational creatures, and a proper object for a man to
love—of course, with that degree and kind of love
which is proper to such an object, and not with silly
anthropomorphic exaggerations—man interferes with
the dog and makes it more lovable than it was in mere
nature. In its state of nature it has a smell, and
habits, which frustrate man's love : he washes it,

house-trains it, teaches it not to steal, and is so enabled to love it completely. To the puppy the whole proceeding would seem, if it were a theologian, to cast grave doubts on the " goodness " of man : but the full-grown and full-trained dog, larger, healthier, and longer-lived than the wild dog, and admitted, as it were by Grace, to a whole world of affections, loyalties, interests, and comforts entirely beyond its animal destiny, would have no such doubts. It will be noted that the man (I am speaking throughout of the good man) takes all these pains with the dog, and gives all these pains to the dog, only because it is an animal high in the scale—because it is so nearly lovable that it is worth his while to make it fully lovable. He does not house-train the earwig or give baths to centipedes. We may wish, indeed, that we were of so little account to God that He left us alone to follow our natural impulses—that He would give over trying to train us into something so unlike our natural selves : but once again, we are asking not for more Love, but for less.

A nobler analogy, sanctioned by the constant tenor of Our Lord's teaching, is that between God's love for man and a father's love for a son. Whenever this is used, however (that is, whenever we pray the Lord's Prayer), it must be remembered that the Saviour used it in a time and place where paternal authority stood much higher than it does in modern England. A father half apologetic for having brought his son into the world, afraid to restrain him lest he should create inhibitions or even to instruct him lest he should interfere with his independence of mind, is a most misleading symbol of the Divine Fatherhood.

I am not here discussing whether the authority of fathers, in its ancient extent, was a good thing or a bad thing : I am only explaining what the conception of Fatherhood would have meant to Our Lord's first hearers, and indeed to their successors for many centuries. And it will become even plainer if we consider how Our Lord (though, in our belief, one with His Father and co-eternal with Him as no earthly son is with an earthly father) regards His own Sonship, surrendering His will wholly to the paternal will and not even allowing Himself to be called "good" because Good is the name of the Father. Love between father and son, in this symbol, means essentially authoritative love on the one side, and obedient love on the other. The father uses his authority to make the son into the sort of human being he, rightly, and in his superior wisdom, wants him to be. Even in our own days, though a man might say, he could mean nothing by saying, " I love my son but don't care how great a blackguard he is provided he has a good time."

Finally we come to an analogy full of danger, and of much more limited application, which happens, nevertheless, to be the most useful for our special purpose at the moment—I mean, the analogy between God's love for man and a man's love for a woman. It is freely used in Scripture. Israel is a false wife, but Her heavenly Husband cannot forget the happier days; "I remember thee, the kindness of thy youth, the love of thy espousals, when thou wentest after Me in the wilderness." [1] Israel is the pauper bride, the waif whom Her lover found abandoned by the

Jer. ii, 2.

wayside, and clothed and adorned and made lovely
and yet she betrayed Him.[1] "Adulteresses" St.
James calls us, because we turn aside to the "friendship
of the world", while God "Jealously longs for the
spirit He has implanted in us".[2] The Church is the
Lord's bride whom He so loves that in her no spot or
wrinkle is endurable.[3] For the truth which this
analogy serves to emphasise is that Love, in its own
nature, demands the perfecting of the beloved; that
the mere "kindness" which tolerates anything
except suffering in its object is, in that respect, at
the opposite pole from Love. When we fall in
love with a woman, do we cease to care whether
she is clean or dirty, fair or foul? Do we not
rather then first begin to care? Does any woman
regard it as a sign of love in a man that he neither
knows nor cares how she is looking? Love may,
indeed, love the beloved when her beauty is lost:
but not because it is lost. Love may forgive all
infirmities and love still in spite of them: but Love
cannot cease to will their removal. Love is more
sensitive than hatred itself to every blemish in the
beloved; his "feeling is more soft and sensible than
are the tender horns of cockled snails". Of all
powers he forgives most, but he condones least: he
is pleased with little, but demands all.

When Christianity says that God loves man, it
means that God *loves* man: not that He has some
"disinterested", because really indifferent, concern
for our welfare, but that, in awful and surprising

---

[1] Ezek. xvi, 6–15.
[2] Jas. iv, 4, 5.   Authorised Version mistranslates.
[3] Eph. v, 27.

truth, we are the objects of His love. You asked for a
loving God : you have one. The great spirit you so
lightly invoked, the " lord of terrible aspect ", is
present : not a senile benevolence that drowsily
wishes you to be happy in your own way, not the
cold philanthropy of a conscientious magistrate, nor
the care of a host who feels responsible for the comfort
of his guests, but the consuming fire Himself, the Love
that made the worlds, persistent as the artist's love
for his work and despotic as a man's love for a dog,
provident and venerable as a father's love for a child,
jealous, inexorable, exacting as love between the
sexes. How this should be, I do not know : it passes
reason to explain why any creatures, not to say
creatures such as we, should have a value so prodigious
in their Creator's eyes. It is certainly a burden of
glory not only beyond our deserts but also, except in
rare moments of grace, beyond our desiring ; we are
inclined, like the maidens in the old play, to deprecate
the love of Zeus.[1] But the fact seems unquestionable.
The Impassible speaks as if it suffered passion, and
that which contains in Itself the cause of its own and
all other bliss talks as though it could be in want and
yearning. " Is Ephraim my dear son ? is he a
pleasant child ? for since I spake against him I do
earnestly remember him still : therefore my bowels
are troubled for him." [2] " How shall I give thee up,
Ephraim ? How shall I abandon thee, Israel ? Mine
heart is turned within me." [3] " Oh Jerusalem, how
often would I have gathered thy children together,

[1] *Prometheus Vinctus*, 887–900.
[2] Jer. xxxi, 20.
[3] Hos. xi, 8.

even as a hen gathereth her chickens under her wings, and ye would not." [1]

The problem of reconciling human suffering with the existence of a God who loves, is only insoluble so long as we attach a trivial meaning to the word " love ", and look on things as if man were the centre of them. Man is not the centre. God does not exist for the sake of man. Man does not exist for his own sake. " Thou hast created all things, and for thy pleasure they are and were created." [2] We were made not primarily that we may love God (though we were made for that too) but that God may love us, that we may become objects in which the Divine love may rest " well pleased ". To ask that God's love should be content with us as we are is to ask that God should cease to be God : because He is what He is, His love must, in the nature of things, be impeded and repelled, by certain stains in our present character, and because He already loves us He must labour to make us lovable. We cannot even wish, in our better moments, that He could reconcile Himself to our present impurities—no more than the beggar maid could wish that King Cophetua should be content with her rags and dirt, or a dog, once having learned to love man, could wish that man were such as to tolerate in his house the snapping, verminous, polluting creature of the wild pack. What we would here and now call our " happiness " is not the end God chiefly has in view : but when we are such as He can love without impediment, we shall in fact be happy.

I plainly foresee that the course of my argument

may provoke a protest. I had promised that in coming to understand the Divine goodness we should not be asked to accept a mere reversal of our own ethics. But it may be objected that a reversal is precisely what we have been asked to accept. The kind of love which I attribute to God, it may be said, is just the kind which in human beings we describe as " selfish " or " possessive ", and contrast unfavourably with another kind which seeks first the happiness of the beloved and not the contentment of the lover. I am not sure that this is quite how I feel even about human love. I do not think I should value much the love of a friend who cared only for my happiness and did not object to my becoming dishonest. Nevertheless, the protest is welcome, and the answer to it will put the subject in a new light, and correct what has been one-sided in our discussion.

The truth is that this antithesis between egoistic and altruistic love cannot be unambiguously applied to the love of God for His creatures. Clashes of interest, and therefore opportunities either of selfishness or unselfishness, occur only between beings inhabiting a common world : God can no more be in competition with a creature than Shakespeare can be in competition with Viola. When God becomes a Man and lives as a creature among His own creatures in Palestine, then indeed His life is one of supreme self-sacrifice and leads to Calvary. A modern pantheistic philosopher has said, " When the Absolute falls into the sea it becomes a fish " ; in the same way, we Christians can point to the Incarnation and say that when God empties Himself of His glory and submits to those conditions under which alone egoism

and altruism have a clear meaning, He is seen to be
wholly altruistic. But God in His transcendence—God
as the unconditioned ground of all conditions—
cannot easily be thought of in the same way. We call
human love selfish when it satisfies its own needs at
the expense of the object's needs—as when a father
keeps at home, because he cannot bear to relinquish
their society, children who ought, in their own
interests, to be put out into the world. The situation
implies a need or passion on the part of the lover, an
incompatible need on the part of the beloved, and
the lover's disregard or culpable ignorance of the
beloved's need. None of these conditions is present
in the relation of God to man. God has no needs.
Human love, as Plato teaches us, is the child of
Poverty—of a want or lack; it is caused by a real
or supposed good in its beloved which the lover
needs and desires. But God's love, far from being
caused by goodness in the object, causes all the
goodness which the object has, loving it first into
existence and then into real, though derivative, love-
ability. God is Goodness. He can give good, but
cannot need or get it. In that sense all His love is, as
it were, bottomlessly selfless by very definition; it
has everything to give and nothing to receive. Hence,
if God sometimes speaks as though the Impassible
could suffer passion and eternal fullness could be in
want, and in want of those beings on whom it bestows
all from their bare existence upwards, this can mean
only, if it means anything intelligible by us, that God
of mere miracle has made Himself able so to hunger
and created in Himself that which we can satisfy. If
He requires us, the requirement is of His own choos-

ing. If the immutable heart can be grieved by the
puppets of its own making, it is Divine Omnipotence,
no other, that has so subjected it, freely, and in a
humility that passes understanding. If the world
exists not chiefly that we may love God but that God
may love us, yet that very fact, on a deeper level, is so
for our sakes. If He who in Himself can lack nothing
chooses to need us, it is because we need to be
needed. Before and behind all the relations of God to
man, as we now learn them from Christianity, yawns
the abyss of a Divine act of pure giving—the election
of man, from nonentity, to be the beloved of God,
and therefore (in some sense) the needed and desired
of God, who but for that act needs and desires
nothing, since He eternally has, and is, all goodness.
And that act is for our sakes. It is good for us to
know love ; and best for us to know the love of the
best object, God. But to know it as a love in which
we were primarily the wooers and God the wooed, in
which we sought and He was found, in which His
conformity to our needs, not ours to His, came first,
would be to know it in a form false to the very nature
of things. For we are only creatures : our *rôle* must
always be that of patient to agent, female to male,
mirror to light, echo to voice. Our highest activity
must be response, not initiative. To experience the
love of God in a true, and not an illusory form, is
therefore to experience it as our surrender to His
demand, our conformity to His desire : to experience
it in the opposite way is, as it were, a solecism against
the grammar of being. I do not deny, of course, that
on a certain level we may rightly speak of the soul's
search for God, and of God as receptive of the soul's

love : but in the long run the soul's search for God can only be a mode, or appearance (*Erscheinung*) of His search for her, since all comes from Him, since the very possibility of our loving is His gift to us, and since our freedom is only a freedom of better or worse response.   Hence I think that nothing marks off Pagan theism from Christianity so sharply as Aristotle's doctrine that God moves the universe, Himself unmoving, as the Beloved moves a lover.[1]   But for Christendom " Herein is love, not that we loved God but that He loved us ".[2]

The first condition, then, of what is called a selfish love among men is lacking with God.   He has no natural necessities, no passion, to compete with His wish for the beloved's welfare : or if there is in Him something which we have to imagine after the analogy of a passion, a want, it is there by His own will and for our sakes.   And the second condition is lacking too.   The real interests of a child may differ from that which his father's affection instinctively demands, because the child is a separate being from the father with a nature which has its own needs and does not exist solely for the father nor find its whole perfection in being loved by him, and which the father does not fully understand.   But creatures are not thus separate from their Creator, nor can He misunderstand them. The place for which He designs them in His scheme of things is the place they are made for.   When they reach it their nature is fulfilled and their happiness attained : a broken bone in the universe has been set, the anguish is over.   When we want to be something

[1] *Met.*, XII, 7.
[2] 1 John iv, 10.

other than the thing God wants us to be, we must be wanting what, in fact, will not make us happy. Those Divine demands which sound to our natural ears most like those of a despot and least like those of a lover, in fact marshall us where we should want to go if we knew what we wanted. He demands our worship, our obedience, our prostration. Do we suppose that they can do Him any good, or fear, like the chorus in Milton, that human irreverence can bring about "His glory's diminution"? A man can no more diminish God's glory by refusing to worship Him than a lunatic can put out the sun by scribbling the word "darkness" on the walls of his cell. But God wills our good, and our good is to love Him (with that responsive love proper to creatures) and to love Him we must know Him : and if we know Him, we shall in fact fall on our faces. If we do not, that only shows that what we are trying to love is not yet God—though it may be the nearest approximation to God which our thought and fantasy can attain. Yet the call is not only to prostration and awe ; it is to a reflection of the Divine life, a creaturely participation in the Divine attributes which is far beyond our present desires. We are bidden to "put on Christ", to become like God. That is, whether we like it or not, God intends to give us what we need, not what we now think we want. Once more, we are embarrassed by the intolerable compliment, by too much love, not too little.

Yet perhaps even this view falls short of the truth. It is not simply that God has arbitrarily made us such that He is our only good. Rather God is the only good of all creatures : and by necessity, each must find its good in that kind and degree of the fruition of God which is proper to its nature. The kind and degree may vary with the creature's nature : but that there ever could be any other good, is an atheistic dream. George Macdonald, in a passage I cannot now find, represents God as saying to men " You must be strong with my strength and blessed with my blessedness, *for I have no other to give you*." That is the conclusion of the whole matter. God gives what He has, not what He has not : He gives the happiness that there is, not the happiness that is not. To be God—to be like God and to share His goodness in creaturely response—to be miserable—these are the only three alternatives. If we will not learn to eat the only food that the universe grows—the only food that any possible universe ever can grow—then we must starve eternally.

IV. HUMAN WICKEDNESS

You can have no greater sign of a confirmed pride than when
you think you are humble enough.

LAW. Serious Call, cap. XVI.

THE examples given in the last chapter went to
show that love may cause pain to its object, but only
on the supposition that that object needs alteration to
become fully lovable. Now why do we men need
so much alteration ? The Christian answer—that we
have used our free will to become very bad—is so
well known that it hardly needs to be stated. But to
bring this doctrine into real life in the minds of
modern men, and even of modern Christians, is very
hard. When the apostles preached, they could
assume even in their Pagan hearers a real consciousness of deserving the Divine anger. The Pagan
mysteries existed to allay this consciousness, and the
Epicurean philosophy claimed to deliver men from
the fear of eternal punishment. It was against this
background that the Gospel appeared as good news.
It brought news of possible healing to men who knew
that they were mortally ill. But all this has changed.
Christianity now has to preach the diagnosis—in
itself very bad news—before it can win a hearing for
the cure.

There are two principal causes. One is the fact
that for about a hundred years we have so concentrated
on one of the virtues—" kindness " or mercy—that

most of us do not feel anything except kindness to be really good or anything but cruelty to be really bad. Such lopsided ethical developments are not uncommon, and other ages too have had their pet virtues and curious insensibilities. And if one virtue must be cultivated at the expense of all the rest, none has a higher claim than mercy—for every Christian must reject with detestation that covert propaganda for cruelty which tries to drive mercy out of the world by calling it names such as " Humanitarianism " and " Sentimentality ". The real trouble is that " kindness " is a quality fatally easy to attribute to ourselves on quite inadequate grounds. Everyone *feels* benevolent if nothing happens to be annoying him at the moment. Thus a man easily comes to console himself for all his other vices by a conviction that " his heart's in the right place " and " he wouldn't hurt a fly ", though in fact he has never made the slightest sacrifice for a fellow creature. We think we are kind when we are only happy : it is not so easy, on the same grounds, to imagine oneself temperate, chaste, or humble.

The second cause is the effect of Psycho-analysis on the public mind, and, in particular, the doctrine of repressions and inhibitions. Whatever these doctrines really mean, the impression they have actually left on most people is that the sense of Shame is a dangerous and mischievous thing. We have laboured to overcome that sense of shrinking, that desire to conceal, which either Nature herself or the tradition of almost all mankind has attached to cowardice, unchastity, falsehood, and envy. We are told to " get things out into the open ", not for the sake of self-humiliation, but on the ground that these "things" are very natural and we need not be ashamed of them. But unless Christianity is wholly false, the perception of ourselves which we have in moments of shame must be the only true one ; and even Pagan society has usually recognised " shamelessness " as the nadir of the soul. In trying to extirpate Shame we have broken down one of the ramparts of the human spirit, madly exulting in the work as the Trojans exulted when they broke their walls and pulled the Horse into Troy. I do not know that there is anything to be done but to set about the rebuilding as soon as we can. It is mad work to remove hypocrisy by removing the *temptation* to hypocrisy : the " frankness " of people, sunk below shame is a very cheap frankness.

A recovery of the old sense of sin is essential to Christianity. Christ takes it for granted that men are bad. Until we really feel this assumption of His to be true, though we are part of the world He came to save, we are not part of the audience to whom His words are addressed. We lack the first condition for understanding what He is talking about. And when men attempt to be Christians without this preliminary consciousness of sin, the result is almost bound to be a certain resentment against God as to one who is always making impossible demands and always inexplicably angry. Most of us have at times felt a secret sympathy with the dying farmer who replied to the Vicar's dissertation on repentance by asking " What harm have I ever done *Him* ? " There is the real rub. The worst we have done to God is to leave Him alone—why can't He return the compliment ?

Why not live and let live? What call has He, of all beings, to be " angry "? It's easy for Him to be good !

Now at the moment whan a man feels real guilt— moments too rare in our lives—all these blasphemies vanish away. Much, we may feel, can be excused to human infirmities : but not *this*—this incredibly mean and ugly action which none of our friends would have done, which even such a thorough-going little rotter as X would have been ashamed of, which we would not for the world allow to be published. At such a moment we really do know that our character, as revealed in this action, is, and ought to be, hateful to all good men, and, if there are powers above man, to them. A God who did not regard this with unappeasable distaste would not be a good being. We cannot even wish for such a God—it is like wishing that every nose in the universe were abolished, that smell of hay or roses or the sea should never again delight any creature, because our own breath happens to stink.

When we merely *say* that we are bad, the " wrath " of God seems a barbarous doctrine ; as soon as we *perceive* our badness, it appears inevitable, a mere corollary from God's goodness. To keep ever before us the insight derived from such a moment as I have been describing, to learn to detect the same real inexcusable corruption under more and more of its complex disguises, is therefore indispensable to a real understanding of the Christian faith. This is not, of course, a new doctrine. I am attempting nothing very splendid in this chapter. I am merely trying to get my reader (and, still more, myself) over a *pons asinorum*—to take the first step out of fools' paradise and utter illusion. But the illusion has grown, in modern times, so strong, that I must add a few considerations tending to make the reality less incredible.

1. We are deceived by looking on the outside of things. We suppose ourselves to be roughly not much worse than Y, whom all acknowledge for a decent sort of person, and certainly (though we should not claim it out loud) better than the abominable X. Even on the superficial level we are probably deceived about this. Don't be too sure that your friends think you as good as Y. The very fact that you selected him for the comparison is suspicious : he is probably head and shoulders above you and your circle. But let us suppose that Y and yourself both appear " not bad ". How far Y's appearance is deceptive, is between Y and God. His may not be deceptive : you know that yours is. Does this seem to you a mere trick, because I could say the same to Y and so to every man in turn ? But that is just the point. Every man, not very holy or very arrogant, has to " live up to " the outward appearance of other men : he knows there is that within him which falls far below even his most careless public behaviour, even his loosest talk. In an instant of time—while your friend hesitates for a word—what things pass through your mind ? We have never told the whole truth. We may confess ugly *facts*—the meanest cowardice or the shabbiest and most prosaic impurity —but the *tone* is false. The very act of confessing— an infinitesimally hypocritical glance—a dash of humour—all this contrives to dissociate the facts

from your very self. No one could guess how familiar and, in a sense, congenial to your soul these things were, how much of a piece with all the rest : down there, in the dreaming inner warmth, they struck no such discordant note, were not nearly so odd and detachable from the rest of you, as they seem when they are turned into words. We imply, and often believe, that habitual vices are exceptional single acts, and make the opposite mistake about our virtues—like the bad tennis player who calls his normal form his " bad days " and mistakes his rare successes for his normal. I do not think it is our fault that we cannot tell the real truth about ourselves ; the persistent, life-long, inner murmur of spite, jealousy, prurience, greed and self-complacence, simply will not go into words. But the important thing is that we should not mistake our inevitably limited utterances for a full account of the worst that is inside.

2. A reaction—in itself wholesome—is now going on against purely private or domestic conceptions of morality, a re-awakening of the *social* conscience. We feel ourselves to be involved in an iniquitous social system and to share a corporate guilt. This is very true : but the enemy can exploit even truths to our deception. Beware lest you are making use of the idea of corporate guilt to distract your attention from those hum-drum, old fashioned guilts of your own which have nothing to do with " the system " and which can be dealt with without waiting for the millennium. For corporate guilt perhaps cannot be, and certainly is not, felt with the same force as personal guilt. For most of us, as we now are, this

conception is a mere excuse for evading the real issue.
When we have really learned to know our individual
corruption, then indeed we can go on to think of the
corporate guilt and can hardly think of it too much.
But we must learn to walk before we run.

3. We have a strange illusion that mere time
cancels sin. I have heard others, and I have heard
myself, recounting cruelties and falsehoods committed
in boyhood as if they were no concern of the present
speaker's, and even with laughter. But mere time
does nothing either to the fact or to the guilt of a sin.
The guilt is washed out not by time but by repentance
and the blood of Christ: if we have repented these
early sins we should remember the price of our
forgiveness and be humble. As for the fact of a sin,
is it probable that anything cancels it? All times are
eternally present to God. Is it not at least possible
that along some one line of His multi-dimensional
eternity He sees you forever in the nursery pulling
the wings off a fly, forever toadying, lying, and
lusting as a schoolboy, forever in that moment of
cowardice or insolence as a subaltern? It may be
that salvation consists not in the cancelling of these
eternal moments but in the perfected humility that
bears the shame forever, rejoicing in the occasion
which it furnished to God's compassion and glad that
it should be common knowledge to the universe.
Perhaps in that eternal moment St. Peter—he will
forgive me if am wrong—forever denies his Master.
If so, it would indeed be true that the joys of Heaven
are for most of us, in our present condition, " an
acquired taste "—and certain ways of life may render
the taste impossible of acquisition. Perhaps the lost

are those who dare not go to such a *public* place. Of course I do not know that this is true; but I think the possibility is worth keeping in mind.

4. We must guard against the feeling that there is " safety in numbers ". It is natural to feel that if *all* men are as bad as the Christians say, then badness must be very excusable. If all the boys plough in the examination, surely the papers must have been too hard ? And so the masters at that school feel till they learn that there are other schools where ninety per cent. of the boys passed on the same papers. Then they begin to suspect that the fault did not lie with the examiners. Again, many of us have had the experience of living in some local pocket of human society—some particular school, college, regiment or profession where the tone was bad. And inside that pocket certain actions were regarded as merely normal (" Everyone does it ") and certain others as impracticably virtuous and Quixotic. But when we emerged from that bad society we made the horrible discovery that in the outer world our " normal " was the kind of thing that no decent person ever dreamed of doing, and our " Quixotic " was taken for granted as the minimum standard of decency. What had seemed to us morbid and fantastic scruples so long as we were in the " pocket " now turned out to be the only moments of sanity we there enjoyed. It is wise to face the possibility that the whole human race (being a small thing in the universe) is, in fact, just such a local pocket of evil—an isolated bad school or regiment inside which minimum decency passes for heroic virtue and utter corruption for pardonable imperfection. But is there any evidence—except

Christian doctrine itself—that this is so? I am afraid there is. In the first place, there are those odd people among us who do not accept the local standard, who demonstrate the alarming truth that a quite different behaviour is, in fact, possible. Worse still, there is the fact that these people, even when separated widely in space and time, have a suspicious knack of agreeing with one another in the main—almost as if they were in touch with some larger public opinion outside the pocket. What is common to Zarathustra, Jeremiah, Socrates, Gotama, Christ [1] and Marcus Aurelius, is something pretty substantial. Thirdly, we find in ourselves even now a theoretical approval of this behaviour which no one practises. Even inside the pocket we do not say that justice, mercy, fortitude, and temperance are of *no* value, but only that the local custom is as just, brave, temperate and merciful as can reasonably be expected. It begins to look as if the neglected school rules even inside this bad school were connected with some larger world—and that when the term ends we might find ourselves facing the public opinion of that larger world. But the worst of all is this ; we cannot help seeing that only the degree of virtue which we now regard as impracticable can possibly save our race from disaster even on this planet. The standard which seems to have come into the " pocket " from outside, turns out to be terribly relevant to conditions inside the pocket—so relevant that a consistent practice of virtue by the human race even for ten years would fill the earth

[1] I mention the Incarnate God among human teachers to emphasise the fact that the *principal* difference between Him and them lies not in ethical teaching (which is here my concern) but in Person and Office.

from pole to pole with peace, plenty, health, merriment, and heartsease, and that nothing else will. It
may be the custom, down here, to treat the regimental
rules as a dead letter or a counsel of perfection : but
even now, everyone who stops to think can see that
when we meet the enemy this neglect is going to cost
every man of us his life. It is then that we shall
envy the " morbid " person, the " pedant " or
" enthusiast " who really *has* taught his company
to shoot and dig in and spare their water bottles.

5. The larger society to which I here contrast the
human " pocket " may not exist according to some
people, and at any rate we have no experience of it.
We do not meet angels, or unfallen races. But we
can get some inkling of the truth even inside our own
race. Different ages and cultures can be regarded as
" pockets " in relation to one another. I said, a few
pages back, that different ages excelled in different
virtues. If, then, you are ever tempted to think that
we modern Western Europeans cannot really be so
very bad because we are, comparatively speaking,
humane—if, in other words, you think God might be
content with us on that ground—ask yourself whether
you think God ought to have been content with the
cruelty of cruel ages because they excelled in courage
or chastity. You will see at once that this is an
impossibility. From considering how the cruelty of
our ancestors looks to us, you may get some inkling
how our softness, worldliness, and timidity would
have looked to them, and hence how both must look
to God.

6. Perhaps my harping on the word " kindness "
has already aroused a protest in some readers' minds,

Are we not really an increasingly cruel age ? Perhaps we are : but I think we have become so in the attempt to reduce all virtues to kindness. For Plato rightly taught that virtue is one. You cannot be kind unless you have all the other virtues. If, being cowardly, conceited and slothful, you have never yet done a fellow creature great mischief, that is only because your neighbour's welfare has not yet happened to conflict with your safety, self-approval, or ease. Every vice leads to cruelty. Even a good emotion, pity, if not controlled by charity and justice, leads through anger to cruelty. Most atrocities are stimulated by accounts of the enemy's atrocities ; and pity for the oppressed classes, when separated from the moral law as a whole, leads by a very natural process to the unremitting brutalities of a reign of terror.

7. Some modern theologians have, quite rightly, protested against an excessively moralistic interpretation of Christianity. The Holiness of God is something more and other than moral perfection : His claim upon us is something more and other than the claim of moral duty. I do not deny it : but this conception, like that of corporate guilt, is very easily used as an evasion of the real issue. God may be more than moral goodness : He is not less. The road to the promised land runs past Sinai. The moral law may exist to be transcended : but there is no transcending it for those who have not first admitted its claims upon them, and then tried with all their strength to meet that claim, and fairly and squarely faced the fact of their failure.

8. " Let no man say when he is tempted, I am

tempted of God." [1]   Many schools of thought
encourage us to shift the responsibility for our
behaviour from our own shoulders to some inherent
necessity in the nature of human life, and thus,
indirectly, to the Creator.   Popular forms of this view
are the evolutionary doctrine that what we call
badness is an unavoidable legacy from our animal
ancestors, or the idealistic doctrine that it is merely
a result of our being finite.   Now Christianity, if I
have understood the Pauline epistles, does admit that
perfect obedience to the moral law, which we find
written in our hearts and perceive to be necessary
even on the biological level, is not in fact possible to
men.   This would raise a real difficulty about our
responsibility if perfect obedience had any practical
relation at all to the lives of most of us.   Some degree
of obedience which you and I have failed to attain
in the last twenty-four hours is certainly possible.
The ultimate problem must not be used as one more
means of evasion.   Most of us are less urgently
concerned with the Pauline question than with
William Law's simple statement : " if you will here
stop and ask yourselves why you are not as pious as
the primitive Christians were, your own heart will
tell you, that it is neither through ignorance nor
inability, but purely because you never thoroughly
intended it." [2]

This chapter will have been misunderstood if
anyone describes it as a reinstatement of the doctrine
of Total Depravity.   I disbelieve that doctrine,
partly on the logical ground that if our depravity

---

[1] Jas. i, 13.
[2] *Serious Call*, cap. 2.

were total we should not know ourselves to be depraved, and partly because experience shows us much goodness in human nature. Nor am I recommending universal gloom. The emotion of shame has been valued not as an emotion but because of the insight to which it leads. I think that insight should be permanent in each man's mind : but whether the painful emotions that attend it should also be encouraged, is a technical problem of spiritual direction on which, as a layman, I have little call to speak. My own idea, for what it is worth, is that all sadness which is not either arising from the repentance of a concrete sin and hastening towards concrete amendment or restitution, or else arising from pity and hastening to active assistance, is simply bad ; and I think we all sin by needlessly disobeying the apostolic injunction to " rejoice " as much as by anything else. Humility, after the first shock, is a cheerful virtue : it is the high-minded unbeliever, desperately trying in the teeth of repeated disillusions to retain his " faith in human nature " who is really sad. I have been aiming at an intellectual, not an emotional, effect : I have been trying to make the reader believe that we actually are, at present, creatures whose character must be, in some respects, a horror to God, as it is, when we really see it, a horror to ourselves. This I believe to be a fact : and I notice that the holier a man is, the more fully he is aware of that fact. Perhaps you have imagined that this humility in the saints is a pious illusion at which God smiles. That is a most dangerous error. It is theoretically dangerous, because it makes you identify a virtue (*i.e.*, a perfection) with an illusion (*i.e.*, an imperfection), which must be nonsense. It is practically dangerous because it encourages a man to mistake his first insights into his own corruption for the first beginnings of a halo round his own silly head. No; depend upon it, when the saints say that they—even they—are vile, they are recording truth with scientific accuracy.

How did this state of affairs come about ? In the next chapter I shall give as much as I can understand of the Christian answer to that question.

V. THE FALL OF MAN

To obey is the proper office of a rational soul.
Montaigne II, xii.

THE Christian answer to the question proposed in the last chapter is contained in the doctrine of the Fall. According to that doctrine, man is now a horror to God and to himself and a creature ill-adapted to the universe not because God made him so but because he has made himself so by the abuse of his free will. To my mind this is the sole function of the doctrine. It exists to guard against two sub-Christian theories of the origin of evil—Monism, according to which God Himself, being "above good and evil", produces impartially the effects to which we give those two names, and Dualism, according to which God produces good, while some equal and independent Power produces evil. Against both these views Christianity asserts that God is good; that He made all things good and for the sake of their goodness; that one of the good things He made, namely, the free will of rational creatures, by its very nature included the possibility of evil; and that creatures, availing themselves of this possibility, have become evil. Now this function—which is the only one I allow to the doctrine of the Fall—must be distinguished from two other functions which it is sometimes, perhaps, represented as performing, but which I reject. In the first place, I do not think the

doctrine answers the question " Was it better for God
to create than not to create ? " That is a question I
have already declined. Since I believe God to be
good, I am sure that, if the question has a meaning,
the answer must be Yes. But I doubt whether the
question has any meaning : and even if it has, I am
sure that the answer cannot be attained by the sort
of value-judgements which men can significantly
make. In the second place, I do not think the doctrine
of the Fall can be used to show that it is " just ", in
terms of retributive justice, to punish individuals for
the faults of their remote ancestors. Some forms of
the doctrine seem to involve this ; but I question
whether any of them, as understood by its exponents,
really meant it. The Fathers may sometimes say
that we are punished for Adam's sin : but they much
more often say that *we* sinned " in Adam ". It may
be impossible to find out what they meant by this, or
we may decide that what they meant was erroneous.
But I do not think we can dismiss their way of talking
as a mere " idiom ". Wisely, or foolishly, they
believed that we were *really*—and not simply by legal
fiction—involved in Adam's action. The attempt to
formulate this belief by saying that we were " in "
Adam in a physical sense—Adam being the first
vehicle of the " immortal germ plasm "—may be
unacceptable : but it is, of course, a further question
whether the belief itself is merely a confusion or a real
insight into spiritual realities beyond our normal
grasp. At the moment, however, this question does
not arise ; for, as I have said I have no intention of
arguing that the descent to modern man of inabilities
contracted by his remote ancestors is a specimen of

retributive justice. For me it is rather a specimen of those things necessarily involved in the creation of a stable world which we considered in Chapter II. It would, no doubt, have been possible for God to remove by miracle the results of the first sin ever committed by a human being; but this would not have been much good unless He was prepared to remove the results of the second sin, and of the third, and so on forever. If the miracles ceased, then sooner or later we might have reached our present lamentable situation: if they did not, then a world, thus continually underpropped and corrected by Divine interference, would have been a world in which nothing important ever depended on human choice, and in which choice itself would soon cease from the certainty that one of the apparent alternatives before you would lead to no results and was therefore not really an alternative. As we saw, the chess player's freedom to play chess depends on the rigidity of the squares and the moves.

Having isolated what I conceive to be the true import of the doctrine that Man is fallen, let us now consider the doctrine in itself. The story in Genesis is a story (full of the deepest suggestion) about a magic apple of knowledge; but in the developed doctrine the inherent magic of the apple has quite dropped out of sight, and the story is simply one of disobedience. I have the deepest respect even for Pagan myths, still more for myths in Holy Scripture. I therefore do not doubt that the version which emphasises the magic apple, and brings together the trees of life and knowledge, contains a deeper and subtler truth than the version which makes the apple simply and solely a pledge of obedience. But I assume that the Holy Spirit would not have allowed the latter to grow up in the Church and win the assent of great doctors unless it also was true and useful as far as it went. It is this version which I am going to discuss, because, though I suspect the primitive version to be far more profound, I know that I, at any rate, cannot penetrate its profundities. I am to give my readers not the best absolutely but the best I have.

In the developed doctrine, then, it is claimed that Man, as God made him, was completely good and completely happy, but that he disobeyed God and became what we now see. Many people think that this proposition has been proved false by modern science. "We now know", it is said, "that so far from having fallen out of a primeval state of virtue and happiness, men have slowly risen from brutality and savagery." There seems to me to be a complete confusion here. *Brute* and *savage* both belong to that unfortunate class of words which are sometimes used rhetorically, as terms of reproach, and sometimes scientifically, as terms of description; and the pseudo-scientific argument against the Fall depends on a confusion between the usages. If by saying that man rose from brutality you mean simply that man is physically descended from animals, I have no objection. But it does not follow that the further back you go the more *brutal*—in the sense of wicked or wretched —you will find man to be. No animal has moral virtue: but it is not true that all animal behaviour is of the kind one should call "wicked" if it were practised by men. On the contrary, not all animals

treat other creatures of their own species as badly as
men treat men. Not all are as gluttonous or lecherous
as we, and no animal is ambitious. Similarly if you
say that the first men were " savages ", meaning by
this that their artefacts were few and clumsy like those
of modern " savages ", you may well be right ; but
if you mean that they were " savage " in the sense of
being lewd, ferocious, cruel, and treacherous, you
will be going beyond your evidence, and that for two
reasons. In the first place, modern anthropologists
and missionaries are less inclined than their fathers
to endorse your unfavourable picture even of the
modern savage. In the second place you cannot argue
from the artefacts of the earliest men that they were
in all respects like the contemporary peoples who
make similar artefacts. We must be on our guard
here against an illusion which the study of prehistoric man seems naturally to beget. Prehistoric
man, because he is prehistoric, is known to us only
by the material things he made—or rather by a chance
selection from among the more durable things he
made. It is not the fault of archæologists that they
have no better evidence : but this penury constitutes
a continual temptation to infer more than we have
any right to infer, to assume that the community
which made the superior artefacts was superior in all
respects. Everyone can see that the assumption is
false ; it would lead to the conclusion that the
leisured classes of our own time were in all respects
superior to those of the Victorian age. Clearly the
prehistoric men who made the worst pottery might
have made the best poetry and we should never know
it. And the assumption becomes even more absurd

when we are comparing prehistoric men with modern savages. The equal crudity of artefacts here tells you nothing about the intelligence or virtue of the makers. What is learned by trial and error must begin by being crude, whatever the character of the beginner. The very same pot which would prove its maker a genius if it were the first pot ever made in the world, would prove its maker a dunce if it came after millenniums of pot-making. The whole modern estimate of primitive man is based upon that idolatry of artefacts which is a great corporate sin of our own civilisation. We forget that our prehistoric ancestors made all the most useful discoveries, except that of chloroform, which have ever been made. To them we owe language, the family, clothing, the use of fire, the domestication of animals, the wheel, the ship, poetry and agriculture.

Science, then, has nothing to say either for or against the doctrine of the Fall. A more philosophical difficulty has been raised by the modern theologian to whom all students of the subject are most indebted.[1] This writer points out that the idea of sin presupposes a law to sin against : and since it would take centuries for the " herd-instinct " to crystallise into custom and for custom to harden into law, the first man—if there ever was a being who could be so described—could not commit the first sin. This argument assumes that virtue and the herd-instinct commonly coincide, and that the " first sin " was essentially a *social* sin. But the traditional doctrine points to a sin against God, an act of disobedience, not a sin against the neighbour. And certainly, if we are to hold the doctrine of the

[1] N. P. Williams. *The Ideas of the Fall and of Original Sin*, p. 516.

Fall in any real sense, we must look for the great sin on a deeper and more timeless level than that of social morality.

This sin has been described by Saint Augustine as the result of Pride, of the movement whereby a creature (that is, an essentially dependent being whose principle of existence lies not in itself but in another) tries to set up on its own, to exist for itself.[1] Such a sin requires no complex social conditions, no extended experience, no great intellectual development. From the moment a creature becomes aware of God as God and of itself as self, the terrible alternative of choosing God or self for the centre is opened to it. This sin is committed daily by young children and ignorant peasants as well as by sophisticated persons, by solitaries no less than by those who live in society: it is the fall in every individual life, and in each day of each individual life, the basic sin behind all particular sins: at this very moment you and I are either committing it, or about to commit it, or repenting it. We try, when we wake, to lay the new day at God's feet; before we have finished shaving, it becomes *our* day and God's share in it is felt as a tribute which we must pay out of " our own " pocket, a deduction from the time which ought, we feel, to be " our own ". A man starts a new job with a sense of vocation and, perhaps, for the first week still keeps the discharge of the vocation as his end, taking the pleasures and pains from God's hand, as they come, as " accidents ". But in the second week he is beginning to " know the ropes ": by the third, he has quarried out of the total job his own plan for

[1] *De Civitate Dei XIV*, xiii.

himself within that job, and when he can pursue this
he feels that he is getting no more than his rights,
and, when he cannot, that he is being interfered with.
A lover, in obedience to a quite uncalculating impulse,
which may be full of good will as well as of desire and
need not be forgetful of God, embraces his beloved,
and then, quite innocently, experiences a thrill of
sexual pleasure; but the second embrace may have
that pleasure in view, may be a means to an end, may
be the first downward step towards the state of
regarding a fellow creature as a thing, as a machine to
be used for his pleasure. Thus the bloom of innocence,
the element of obedience and the readiness to take
what comes is rubbed off every activity. Thoughts
undertaken for God's sake—like that on which we
are engaged at the moment—are continued as if they
were an end in themselves, and then as if our pleasure
in thinking were the end, and finally as if our pride
or celebrity were the end. Thus all day long, and
all the days of our life, we are sliding, slipping, falling
away—as if God were, to our present consciousness,
a smooth inclined plane on which there is no resting.
And indeed we are now of such a nature that we must
slip off, and the sin, because it is unavoidable, may be
venial. But God cannot have made us so. The
gravitation away from God, " the journey homeward
to habitual self ", must, we think, be a product of the
Fall. What exactly happened when Man fell, we do
not know; but if it is legitimate to guess, I offer the
following picture—a " myth " in the Socratic sense,[1]
a not unlikely tale.

---

[1] *I.e.*, an account of what *may have been* the historical fact. Not to be
confused with " myth " in Dr. Niebuhr's sense (*i.e.*, a symbolical
representation of non-historical truth).

For long centuries God perfected the animal form which was to become the vehicle of humanity and the image of Himself. He gave it hands whose thumb could be applied to each of the fingers, and jaws and teeth and throat capable of articulation, and a brain sufficiently complex to execute all the material motions whereby rational thought is incarnated. The creature may have existed for ages in this state before it became man : it may even have been clever enough to make things which a modern archæologist would accept as proof of its humanity. But it was only an animal because all its physical and psychical processes were directed to purely material and natural ends. Then, in the fullness of time, God caused to descend upon this organism, both on its psychology and physiology, a new kind of consciousness which could say " I " and " me ", which could look upon itself as an object, which knew God, which could make judgements of truth, beauty, and goodness, and which was so far above time that it could perceive time flowing past. This new consciousness ruled and illuminated the whole organism, flooding every part of it with light, and was not, like ours, limited to a selection of the movements going on in one part of the organism, namely the brain. Man was then all consciousness. The modern Yogi claims—whether falsely or truly—to have under control those functions which to us are almost part of the external world, such as digestion and circulation. This power the first man had in eminence. His organic processes obeyed the law of his own will, not the law of nature. His organs sent up appetites to the judgement seat of will not because they had to, but because he chose.

Sleep meant to him not the stupor which we undergo, but willed and conscious repose—he remained awake to enjoy the pleasure and duty of sleep. Since the processes of decay and repair in his tissues were similarly conscious and obedient, it may not be fanciful to suppose that the length of his life was largely at his own discretion. Wholly commanding himself, he commanded all lower lives with which he came into contact. Even now we meet rare individuals who have a mysterious power of taming beasts. This power the Paradisal man enjoyed in eminence. The old picture of the brutes sporting before Adam and fawning upon him may not be wholly symbolical. Even now more animals than you might expect are ready to adore man if they are given a reasonable opportunity : for man was made to be the priest and even, in one sense, the Christ, of the animals—the mediator through whom they apprehend so much of the Divine splendour as their irrational nature allows. And God was to such a man no slippery, inclined plane. The new consciousness had been made to repose on its Creator, and repose it did. However rich and varied man's experience of his fellows (or fellow) in charity and friendship and sexual love, or of the beasts, or of the surrounding world then first recognised as beautiful and awful, God came first in his love and in his thought, and that without painful effort. In perfect cyclic movement, being, power and joy descended from God to man in the form of gift and returned from man to God in the form of obedient love and ecstatic adoration : and in this sense, though not in all, man was then truly the son of God, the prototype of Christ, perfectly enacting in joy and ease of all the faculties and all the senses that filial self-surrender which Our Lord enacted in the agonies of the crucifixion.

Judged by his artefacts, or perhaps even by his language, this blessed creature was, no doubt, a savage. All that experience and practice can teach he had still to learn : if he chipped flints, he doubtless chipped them clumsily enough. He may have been utterly incapable of expressing in conceptual form his paradisal experience. All that is quite irrelevant. From our own childhood we remember that before our elders thought us capable of " understanding " anything, we already had spiritual experiences as pure and as momentous as any we have undergone since, though not, of course, as rich in factual context. From Christianity itself we learn that there is a level— in the long run the only level of importance—on which the learned and the adult have no advantage at all over the simple and the child. I do not doubt that if the Paradisal man could now appear among us, we should regard him as an utter savage, a creature to be exploited or, at best, patronised. Only one or two, and those the holiest among us, would glance a second time at the naked, shaggy-bearded, slow-spoken creature : but they, after a few minutes, would fall at his feet.

We do not know how many of these creatures God made, nor how long they continued in the Paradisal state. But sooner or later they fell. Someone or something whispered that they could become as gods —that they could cease directing their lives to their Creator and taking all their delights as uncovenanted mercies, as " accidents " (in the logical sense) which

arose in the course of a life directed not to those
delights but to the adoration of God. As a young man
wants a regular allowance from his father which he
can count on as his own, within which he makes his
own plans (and rightly, for his father is after all a
fellow creature) so they desired to be on their own,
to take care for their own future, to plan for pleasure
and for security, to have a *meum* from which, no
doubt, they would pay some reasonable tribute to
God in the way of time, attention, and love, but which
nevertheless, was theirs not His. They wanted, as
we say, to " call their souls their own ". But that
means to live a lie, for our souls are not, in fact, our
own. They wanted some corner in the universe of
which they could say to God, " This is our business,
not yours." But there is no such corner. They
wanted to be nouns, but they were, and eternally
must be, mere adjectives. We have no idea in what
particular act, or series of acts, the self-contradictory,
impossible wish found expression. For all I can see,
it might have concerned the literal eating of a fruit,
but the question is of no consequence.

This act of self-will on the part of the creature,
which constitutes an utter falseness to its true
creaturely position, is the only sin that can be con-
ceived as the Fall. For the difficulty about the first
sin is that it must be very heinous, or its consequences
would not be so terrible, and yet it must be something
which a being free from the temptations of fallen man
could conceivably have committed. The turning from
God to self fulfills both conditions. It is a sin possible
even to Paradisal man, because the mere existence of
a self—the mere fact that we call it " me "—includes,

from the first, the danger of self-idolatry. Since I am I, I must make an act of self-surrender, however small or however easy, in living to God rather than to myself. This is, if you like, the " weak spot " in the very nature of creation, the risk which God apparently thinks worth taking. But the sin was very heinous, because the self which Paradisal man had to surrender contained no natural recalcitrancy to being surrendered. His *data*, so to speak, were a psycho-physical organism wholly subject to the will and a will wholly disposed, though not compelled, to turn to God. The self-surrender which he practised before the Fall meant no struggle but only the delicious overcoming of an infinitesimal self-adherence which delighted to be overcome—of which we see a dim analogy in the rapturous mutual self-surrenders of lovers even now. He had, therefore, no *temptation* (in our sense) to choose the self—no passion or inclination obstinately inclining that way—nothing but the bare fact that the self was *him*self.

Up to that moment the human spirit had been in full control of the human organism. It doubtless expected that it would retain this control when it had ceased to obey God. But its authority over the organism was a delegated authority which it lost when it ceased to be God's delegate. Having cut itself off, as far as it could, from the source of its being, it had cut itself off from the source of power. For when we say of created things that A rules B this must mean that God rules B through A. I doubt whether it would have been intrinsically possible for God to continue to rule the organism *through* the human spirit when the human spirit was in revolt against

Him. At any rate He did not. He began to rule the
organism in a more external way, not by the laws of
spirit, but by those of nature.[1] Thus the organs, no
longer governed by man's will, fell under the control
of ordinary biochemical laws and suffered whatever
the inter-workings of those laws might bring about
in the way of pain, senility and death. And desires
began to come up into the mind of man, not as his
reason chose, but just as the biochemical and environ-
mental facts happened to cause them. And the mind
itself fell under the psychological laws of association
and the like which God had made to rule the
psychology of the higher anthropoids. And the will,
caught in the tidal wave of mere nature, had no
resource but to force back some of the new thoughts
and desires by main strength, and these uneasy rebels
became the subconscious as we now know it. The
process was not, I conceive, comparable to mere
deterioration as it may now occur in a human
individual; it was a loss of status as a *species*. What
man lost by the Fall was his original specific nature.
" Dust thou art, and unto dust shalt thou return."
The total organism which had been taken up into his
spiritual life was allowed to fall back into the merely
natural condition from which, at his making, it had
been raised—just as, far earlier in the story of creation,
God had raised vegetable life to become the vehicle
of animality, and chemical process to be the vehicle
of vegetation, and physical process to be the vehicle

[1] This is a development of Hooker's conception of Law. To disobey
your *proper* law (*i.e.*, the law God makes for a being such as *you*) means
to find yourself obeying one of God's lower laws : *e.g.*, if, when walking
on a slippery pavement, you neglect the law of Prudence, you suddenly
find yourself obeying the law of gravitation.

of chemical. Thus human spirit from being the master of human nature became a mere lodger in its own house, or even a prisoner; rational consciousness became what it now is—a fitful spot-light resting on a small part of the cerebral motions. But this limitation of the spirit's powers was a lesser evil than the corruption of the spirit itself. It had turned from God and become its own idol, so that though it could still turn back to God,[1] it could do so only by painful effort, and its inclination was self-ward. Hence pride and ambition, the desire to be lovely in its own eyes and to depress and humiliate all rivals, envy, and restless search for more, and still more, security, were now the attitudes that came easiest to it. It was not only a weak king over its own nature, but a bad one: it sent down into the psycho-physical organism desires far worse than the organism sent up in to it. This condition was transmitted by heredity to all later generations, for it was not simply what biologists call an acquired variation; it was the emergence of a new kind of man—a new species, never made by God, had sinned itself into existence. The change which man had undergone was not parallel to the development of a new organ or a new habit; it was a radical alteration of his constitution, a disturbance of the relation between his component parts, and an internal perversion of one of them.

God might have arrested this process by miracle: but this—to speak in somewhat irreverent metaphor—

[1] Theologians will note that I am not here intending to make any contribution to the Pelagian-Augustinian controversy. I mean only that such return to God was not, even now, an impossibility. Where the initiative lies in any instance of such return is a question on which I am saying nothing.

would have been to decline the problem which God had set Himself when He created the world, the problem of expressing His goodness through the total drama of a world containing free agents, in spite of, and by means of, their rebellion against Him. The symbol of a drama, a symphony, or a dance, is here useful to correct a certain absurdity which may arise if we talk too much of God planning and creating the world process for good and of that good being frustrated by the free will of the creatures. This may raise the ridiculous idea that the Fall took God by surprise and upset His plan, or else—more ridiculously still—that God planned the whole thing for conditions which, He well knew, were never going to be realised. In fact, of course, God saw the crucifixion in the act of creating the first nebula. The world is a dance in which good, descending from God, is disturbed by evil arising from the creatures, and the resulting conflict is resolved by God's own assumption of the suffering nature which evil produces. The doctrine of the free Fall asserts that the evil which thus makes the fuel or raw material for the second and more complex kind of good is not God's contribution but man's. This does not mean that if man had remained innocent God could not then have contrived an equally splendid symphonic whole—supposing that we insist on asking such questions. But it must always be remembered that when we talk of what might have happened, of contingencies outside the whole actuality, we do not really know what we are talking about. There are no times or places outside the existing universe in which all this " could happen " or " could have happened ", I think the most

significant way of stating the real freedom of man is
to say that if there are other rational species than man,
existing in some other part of the actual universe, then
it is not necessary to suppose that they also have
fallen.

Our present condition, then, is explained by the
fact that we are members of a spoiled species. I do
not mean that our sufferings are a punishment for
being what we cannot now help being nor that we
are morally responsible for the rebellion of a remote
ancestor. If, none the less, I call our present condition
one of original Sin, and not merely one of original
misfortune, that is because our actual religious
experience does not allow us to regard it in any other
way. Theoretically, I suppose, we might say " Yes :
we behave like vermin, but then that is because we
are vermin. And that, at any rate, is not our fault."
But the fact that we are vermin, so far from being felt
as an excuse, is a greater shame and grief to us than
any of the particular acts which it leads us to commit.
The situation is not nearly so hard to understand as
some people make out. It arises among human beings
whenever a very badly brought up boy is introduced
into a decent family. They rightly remind themselves
that it is " not his own fault " that he is a bully, a
coward, a tale-bearer and a liar. But none the less,
however it came there, his present character is
detestable. They not only hate it, but ought to hate
it. They cannot love him for what he is, they can
only try to turn him into what he is not. In the
meantime, though the boy is most unfortunate in
having been so brought up, you cannot quite call his
character a " misfortune " as if he were one thing and

his character another. It is he—he himself—who
bullies and sneaks and likes doing it. And if he begins
to mend he will inevitably feel shame and guilt at what
he is just beginning to cease to be.

With this I have said all that can be said on the level
at which alone I feel able to treat the subject of the
Fall. But I warn my readers once more that this level
is a shallow one. We have said nothing about the
trees of life and of knowledge which doubtless conceal
some great mystery : and we have said nothing about
the Pauline statement that " as in Adam all die, so in
Christ shall all be made alive ". [1] It is this passage
which lies behind the Patristic doctrine of our physical
presence in Adam's loins and Anselm's doctrine of our
inclusion, by legal fiction, in the suffering Christ.
These theories may have done good in their day but
they do no good to me, and I am not going to invent
others. We have recently been told by the scientists
that we have no right to expect that the real universe
should be picturable, and that if we make mental
pictures to illustrate quantum physics we are moving
further away from reality, not nearer to it. [2] We have
clearly even less right to demand that the highest
spiritual realities should be picturable, or even
explicable in terms of our abstract thought. I observe
that the difficulty of the Pauline formula turns on the
word *in*, and that this word, again and again in the
New Testament, is used in senses we cannot fully
understand. That we can die " in " Adam and live
" in " Christ seems to me to imply that man, as he
really is, differs a good deal from man as our categories

[1] 1 Cor. xv, 22.
[2] Sir James Jeans' *The Mysterious Universe*, cap. 5.

THE FALL OF MAN

of thought and our three dimensional imaginations represent him ; that the separateness—modified only by causal relations—which we discern between individuals, is balanced, in absolute reality, by some kind of " inter-inanimation " of which we have no conception at all. It may be that the acts and sufferings of great archetypal individuals such as Adam and Christ are ours, not by legal fiction, metaphor, or causality, but in some much deeper fashion. There is no question, of course, of individuals melting down into a kind of spiritual continuum such as Pantheistic systems believe in ; that is excluded by the whole tenor of our faith. But there may be a tension between individuality and some other principle. We believe that the Holy Spirit can be really present and operative in the human spirit, but we do not, like Pantheists, take this to mean that we are " parts " or " modifications " or " appearances " of God. We may have to suppose, in the long run, that something of the same kind is true, in its appropriate degree, even of created spirits, that each, though distinct, is really present in all, or in some, others—just as we may have to admit " action at a distance " into our conception of matter. Everyone will have noticed how the Old Testament seems at times to ignore our conception of the individual. When God promises Jacob that " He will go down with him into Egypt and will also surely bring him up again ", [1] this is fulfilled either by the burial of Jacob's body in Palestine or by the exodus of Jacob's descendants from Egypt. It is quite right to connect this notion with the social structure of early communities in

[1] Gen. xlvi, 4.

which the individual is constantly overlooked in favour of the tribe or family : but we ought to express this connection by two propositions of equal importance—firstly that their social experience blinded the ancients to some truths which we perceive, and secondly that it made them sensible of some truths to which we are blind. Legal fiction, adoption, and transference or imputation of merit and guilt, could never have played the part they did play in theology if they had always been felt to be so artificial as we now feel them to be.

I have thought it right to allow this one glance at what is for me an impenetrable curtain, but, as I have said, it makes no part of my present argument. Clearly it would be futile to attempt to solve the problem of pain by producing another problem. The thesis of this chapter is simply that man, as a species, spoiled himself, and that good, to us in our present state, must therefore mean primarily remedial or corrective good. What part pain actually plays in such remedy or correction, is now to be considered.

VI. HUMAN PAIN

Since the life of Christ is every way most bitter to nature and the Self and the Me (for in the true life of Christ, the Self and the Me and nature must be forsaken and lost and die altogether), therefore in each of us, nature hath a horror of it.

Theologia Germanica, XX.

I HAVE tried to show in a previous chapter that the possibility of pain is inherent in the very existence of a world where souls can meet. When souls become wicked they will certainly use this possibility to hurt one another; and this, perhaps, accounts for four-fifths of the sufferings of men. It is men, not God, who have produced racks, whips, prisons, slavery, guns, bayonets, and bombs; it is by human avarice or human stupidity, not by the churlishness of nature, that we have poverty and overwork. But there remains, none the less, much suffering which cannot thus be traced to ourselves. Even if all suffering were man-made, we should like to know the reason for the enormous permission to torture their fellows which God gives to the worst of men.[1] To say, as was said in the last chapter, that good, for such creatures as we now are, means

---

[1] Or perhaps it would be safer to say " of creatures ". I by no means reject the view that the " efficient cause " of disease, or some disease, may be a created being other than man (see Chapter IX). In Scripture Satan is specially associated with disease in Job, in Luke xiii, 16, 1 Cor. v, 5, and (probably) in 1 Tim. i, 20. It is, at the present stage of the argument, indifferent whether all the created wills to which God allows a power of tormenting other creatures are human or not.

primarily corrective or remedial good, is an incomplete answer. Not all medicine tastes nasty : or if it did, that is itself one of the unpleasant facts for which we should like to know the reason.

Before proceeding I must pick up a point made in Chapter II. I there said that pain, below a certain level of intensity, was not resented and might even be rather liked. Perhaps you then wanted to reply " In that case I should not call it Pain ", and you may have been right. But the truth is that the word Pain has two senses which must now be distinguished. A. A particular kind of sensation, probably conveyed by specialised nerve fibres, and recognisable by the patient as that kind of sensation whether he dislikes it or not (e.g., the faint ache in my limbs would be recognised as an ache even if I didn't object to it). B. Any experience, whether physical or mental, which the patient dislikes. It will be noticed that all Pains in sense A become Pains in sense B if they are raised above a certain very low level of intensity, but that Pains in the B sense need not be Pains in the A sense. Pain in the B sense, in fact, is synonymous with " suffering ", " anguish ", " tribulation ", " adversity ", or " trouble ", and it is about it that the problem of pain arises. For the rest of this book Pain will be used in the B sense and will include all types of suffering : with the A sense we have no further concern.

Now the proper good of a creature is to surrender itself to its Creator—to enact intellectually, volitionally, and emotionally, that relationship which is given in the mere fact of its being a creature. When it does so, it is good and happy. Lest we should think this a hardship, this kind of good begins on a level far above the creatures, for God Himself, as Son, from all eternity renders back to God as Father by filial obedience the being which the Father by paternal love eternally generates in the Son. This is the pattern which man was made to imitate—which Paradisal man did imitate—and wherever the will conferred by the Creator is thus perfectly offered back in delighted and delighting obedience by the creature, there, most undoubtedly, is Heaven, and there the Holy Ghost proceeds. In the world as we now know it, the problem is how to recover this self-surrender. We are not merely imperfect creatures who must be improved : we are, as Newman said, rebels who must lay down our arms. The first answer, then, to the question why our cure should be painful, is that to render back the will which we have so long claimed for our own, is in itself, wherever and however it is done, a grievous pain. Even in Paradise I have supposed a minimal self-adherence to be overcome, though the overcoming, and the yielding, would there be rapturous. But to surrender a self-will inflamed and swollen with years of usurpation is a kind of death. We all remember this self-will as it was in childhood the bitter, prolonged rage at every thwarting, the burst of passionate tears, the black, Satanic wish to kill or die rather than to give in. Hence the older type of nurse or parent was quite right in thinking that the first step in education is " to break the child's will ". Their methods were often wrong : but not to see the necessity is, I think, to cut oneself off from all understanding of spiritual laws. And if, now that we are grown up, we do not howl and stamp

quite so much, that is partly because our elders began
the process of breaking or killing our self-will in the
nursery, and partly because the same passions now
take more subtle forms and have grown clever at
avoiding death by various " compensations ". Hence
the necessity to die daily : however often we think we
have broken the rebellious self we shall still find it
alive. That this process cannot be without pain is
sufficiently witnessed by the very history of the word
" Mortification ".

But this intrinsic pain, or death, in mortifying the
usurped self, is not the whole story. Paradoxically,
mortification, though itself a pain, is made easier by
the presence of pain in its context. This happens, I
think, principally in three ways.

The human spirit will not even begin to try to
surrender self-will as long as all seems to be well with
it. Now error and sin both have this property, that
the deeper they are the less their victim suspects their
existence ; they are masked evil. Pain is unmasked,
unmistakable evil ; every man knows that something
is wrong when he is being hurt. The Masochist is no
real exception. Sadism and Masochism respectively
isolate, and then exaggerate, a " moment " or
" aspect " in normal sexual passion. Sadism [1]
exaggerates the aspect of capture and domination to a
point at which only ill-treatment of the beloved will
satisfy the pervert—as though he said, " I am so
much master that I even torment you." Masochism
exaggerates the complementary and opposite aspect,
and says " I am so enthralled that I welcome even

---

[1] The modern tendency to mean by " sadistic cruelty " simply " great
cruelty ", or cruelty specially condemned by the writer, is not useful.

pain at your hands ". Unless the pain were felt as evil—as an outrage underlining the complete mastery of the other party—it would cease, for the Masochist, to be an erotic stimulus. And pain is not only immediately recognisable evil, but evil impossible to ignore. We can rest contentedly in our sins and in our stupidities; and anyone who has watched gluttons shovelling down the most exquisite foods as if they did not know what they were eating, will admit that we can ignore even pleasure. But pain insists upon being attended to. God whispers to us in our pleasures, speaks in our conscience, but shouts in our pains: it is His megaphone to rouse a deaf world. A bad man, happy, is a man without the least inkling that his actions do not " answer ", that they are not in accord with the laws of the universe.

A perception of this truth lies at the back of the universal human feeling that bad men ought to suffer. It is no use turning up our noses at this feeling, as if it were wholly base. On its mildest level it appeals to everyone's sense of justice. Once when my brother and I, as very small boys, were drawing pictures at the same table, I jerked his elbow and caused him to make an irrelevant line across the middle of his work ; the matter was amicably settled by my allowing him to draw a line of equal length across mine. That is, I was " put in his place ", made to see my negligence from the other end. On a sterner level the same idea appears as " retributive punishment ", or " giving a man what he deserves ". Some enlightened people would like to banish all conceptions of retribution or desert from their theory of punishment and place its value wholly in the deterrence of others or the reform of the criminal himself. They do not see that by so doing they render all punishment unjust. What can be more immoral than to inflict suffering on me for the sake of deterring others if I do not *deserve* it? And if I do deserve it, you are admitting the claims of "retribution". And what can be more outrageous than to catch me and submit me to a disagreeable process of moral improvement without my consent, unless (once more) I *deserve* it? On yet a third level we get vindictive passion—the thirst for revenge. This, of course, is evil and expressly forbidden to Christians. But it has perhaps appeared already from our discussion of Sadism and Masochism that the ugliest things in human nature are perversions of good or innocent things. The good thing of which vindictive passion is the perversion comes out with startling clarity in Hobbes's definition of Revengefulness; "desire by doing hurt to another to make him condemn some fact of his own".[1] Revenge loses sight of the end in the means, but its end is not wholly bad—it wants the evil of the bad man to be to him what it is to everyone else. This is proved by the fact that the avenger wants the guilty party not merely to suffer, but to suffer at his hands, and to know it, and to know why. Hence the impulse to taunt the guilty man with his crime at the moment of taking vengeance: hence, too, such natural expressions as "I wonder how he'd like it if the same thing were done to him" or "I'll teach him". For the same reason when we are going to abuse a man in words we say we are going to "let him know what we think of him".

[1] *Leviathan*, Pt. I, cap. 6.

When our ancestors referred to pains and sorrows as God's "vengeance" upon sin they were not necessarily attributing evil passions to God; they may have been recognising the good element in the idea of retribution. Until the evil man finds evil unmistakably present in his existence, in the form of pain, he is enclosed in illusion. Once pain has roused him, he knows that he is in some way or other "up against" the real universe: he either rebels (with the possibility of a clearer issue and deeper repentance at some later stage) or else makes some attempt at an adjustment, which, if pursued, will lead him to religion. It is true that neither effect is so certain now as it was in ages when the existence of God (or even of the Gods) was more widely known, but even in our own days we see it operating. Even atheists rebel and express, like Hardy and Housman, their rage against God although (or because) He does not, on their view, exist: and other atheists, like Mr. Huxley, are driven by suffering to raise the whole problem of existence and to find some way of coming to terms with it which, if not Christian, is almost infinitely superior to fatuous contentment with a profane life. No doubt Pain as God's megaphone is a terrible instrument; it may lead to final and un-repented rebellion. But it gives the only opportunity the bad man can have for amendment. It removes the veil; it plants the flag of truth within the fortress of a rebel soul.

If the first and lowest operation of pain shatters the illusion that all is well, the second shatters the illusion that what we have, whether good or bad in itself, is our own and enough for us. Everyone has noticed how hard it is to turn our thoughts to God when everything is going well with us. We " have all we want " is a terrible saying when " all " does not include God. We find God an interruption. As St. Augustine says somewhere " God wants to give us something, but cannot, because our hands are full— there's nowhere for Him to put it." Or as a friend of mine said " we regard God as an airman regards his parachute ; it's there for emergencies but he hopes he'll never have to use it." Now God, who has made us, knows what we are and that our happiness lies in Him. Yet we will not seek it in Him as long as He leaves us any other resort where it can even plausibly be looked for. While what we call " our own life " remains agreeable we will not surrender it to Him. What then can God do in our interests but make " our own life " less agreeable to us, and take away the plausible sources of false happiness ? It is just here, where God's providence seems at first to be most cruel, that the Divine humility, the stooping down of the Highest, most deserves praise. We are perplexed to see misfortune falling upon decent, inoffensive, worthy people—on capable, hard-working mothers of families or diligent, thrifty, little trades-people, on those who have worked so hard, and so honestly, for their modest stock of happiness and now seem to be entering on the enjoyment of it with the fullest right. How can I say with sufficient tenderness what here needs to be said ? It does not matter that I know I must become, in the eyes of every hostile reader, as it were personally responsible for all the sufferings I try to explain—just as, to this day, everyone talks as if St. Augustine *wanted* unbaptised infants to go to

Hell. But it matters enormously if I alienate anyone
from the truth. Let me implore the reader to try to
believe, if only for the moment, that God, who made
these deserving people, may really be right when He
thinks that their modest prosperity and the happiness
of their children are not enough to make them blessed :
that all this must fall from them in the end, and that
if they have not learned to know Him they will be
wretched. And therefore He troubles them, warning
them in advance of an insufficiency that one day they
will have to discover. The life to themselves and their
families stands between them and the recognition of
their need ; He makes that life less sweet to them. I
call this a Divine humility because it is a poor thing
to strike our colours to God when the ship is going
down under us ; a poor thing to come to Him as a last
resort, to offer up " our own " when it is no longer
worth keeping. If God were proud He would hardly
have us on such terms : but He is not proud, He stoops
to conquer, He will have us even though we have
shown that we prefer everything else to Him, and come
to Him because there is " nothing better " now to
be had. The same humility is shown by all those
Divine appeals to our fears which trouble high-
minded readers of scripture. It is hardly compli-
mentary to God that we should choose Him as an
alternative to Hell : yet even this He accepts. The
creature's illusion of self-sufficiency must, for the
creature's sake, be shattered ; and by trouble or fear
of trouble on earth, by crude fear of the eternal
flames, God shatters it " unmindful of His glory's
diminution ". Those who would like the God of
scripture to be more purely ethical, do not know what

they ask. If God were a Kantian, who would not
have us till we came to Him from the purest and best
motives, who could be saved ? And this illusion of
self-sufficiency may be at its strongest in some very
honest, kindly, and temperate people, and on such
people, therefore, misfortune must fall.

The dangers of apparent self-sufficiency explain
why Our Lord regards the vices of the feckless and
dissipated so much more leniently than the vices that
lead to worldly success. Prostitutes are in no danger
of finding their present life so satisfactory that they
cannot turn to God : the proud, the avaricious, the
self-righteous, are in that danger.

The third operation of suffering is a little harder to
grasp. Everyone will admit that choice is essentially
conscious ; to choose involves knowing that you
choose. Now Paradisal man always chose to follow
God's will. In following it he also gratified his own
desire, both because all the actions demanded of him
were, in fact, agreeable to his blameless inclination,
and also because the service of God was itself his
keenest pleasure, without which as their razor edge
all joys would have been insipid to him. The
question " Am I doing this for God's sake or only
because I happen to like it ? " did not then arise,
since doing things for God's sake was what he
chiefly " happened to like ". His God-ward will rode
his happiness like a well-managed horse, whereas our
will, when we are happy, is carried away in the
happiness as in a ship racing down a swift stream.
Pleasure was then an acceptable offering to God
because offering was a pleasure. But we inherit a
whole system of desires which do not necessarily

contradict God's will but which, after centuries of
usurped autonomy, steadfastly ignore it. If the thing
we like doing is, in fact, the thing God wants us to do,
yet that is not our reason for doing it; it remains a
mere happy coincidence. We cannot therefore know
that we are acting at all, or primarily, for God's sake,
unless the material of the action is contrary to our
inclinations, or (in other words) painful, and what
we cannot know that we are choosing, we cannot
choose. The full acting out of the self's surrender to
God therefore demands pain: this action, to be
perfect, must be done from the pure will to obey, in
the absence, or in the teeth, of inclination. How
impossible it is to enact the surrender of the self by
doing what we like, I know very well from my own
experience at the moment. When I undertook to
write this book I hoped that the will to obey what
might be a " leading " had at least some place in my
motives. But now that I am thoroughly immersed
in it, it has become a temptation rather than a duty.
I may still hope that the writing of the book is, in
fact, in conformity with God's will: but to contend
that I am learning to surrender myself by doing what
is so attractive to me would be ridiculous.

Here we tread on very difficult ground. Kant
thought that no action had moral value unless it were
done out of pure reverence for the moral law, that is,
without inclination, and he has been accused of a
" morbid frame of mind " which measures the value
of an act by its unpleasantness. All popular opinion
is, indeed, on Kant's side. The people never admire
a man for doing something he likes: the very words
" But he *likes* it " imply the corollary " And therefore

it has no merit ". Yet against Kant stands the obvious truth, noted by Aristotle, that the more virtuous a man becomes the more he enjoys virtuous actions. What an atheist ought to do about this conflict between the ethics of duty and the ethics of virtue, I do not know : but as a Christian I suggest the following solution.

It has sometimes been asked whether God commands certain things because they are right, or whether certain things are right because God commands them. With Hooker, and against Dr. Johnson, I emphatically embrace the first alternative. The second might lead to the abominable conclusion (reached, I think, by Paley) that charity is good only because God arbitrarily commanded it—that He might equally well have commanded us to hate Him and one another and that hatred would then have been right. I believe, on the contrary, that " they err who think that of the will of God to do this or that there is no reason besides His will ".[1] God's will is determined by His wisdom which always perceives, and His goodness which always embraces, the intrinsically good. But when we have said that God commands things only because they are good, we must add that one of the things intrinsically good is that rational creatures should freely surrender themselves to their Creator in obedience. The content of our obedience—the thing we are commanded to do— will always be something intrinsically good, something we ought to do even if (by an impossible supposition) God had not commanded it. But in addition to the content, the mere obeying is also

[1] Hooker. *Laws of Eccl. Polity*, I, i, 5.

intrinsically good, for, in obeying, a rational creature
consciously enacts its creaturely *rôle*, reverses the
act by which we fell, treads Adam's dance backward,
and returns.

We therefore agree with Aristotle that what is
intrinsically right may well be agreeable, and that the
better a man is the more he will like it ; but we agree
with Kant so far as to say that there is one right act—
that of self surrender—which cannot be willed to the
height by fallen creatures unless it is unpleasant. And
we must add that this one right act includes all other
righteousness, and that the supreme cancelling of
Adam's fall, the movement " full speed astern " by
which we retrace our long journey from Paradise, the
untying of the old, hard knot, must be when the
creature, with no desire to aid it, stripped naked to
the bare willing of obedience, embraces what is
contrary to its nature, and does that for which only
one motive is possible. Such an act may be described
as a " test " of the creature's return to God : hence
our fathers said that troubles were " sent to try us ".
A familiar example is Abraham's " trial " when he was
ordered to sacrifice Isaac. With the historicity or the
morality of that story I am not now concerned, but
with the obvious question " If God is omniscient He
must have known what Abraham would do, without
any experiment ; why, then, this needless torture ? "
But as St. Augustine points out,[1] whatever God knew,
Abraham at any rate did not know that his obedience
could endure such a command until the event taught
him : and the obedience which he did not know that
he would choose, he cannot be said to have chosen,

[1] *De Civitate Dei*, XVI, xxxii.

The reality of Abraham's obedience was the act
itself; and what God knew in knowing that Abraham
" would obey " was Abraham's actual obedience on
that mountain top at that moment. To say that God
" need not have tried the experiment " is to say that
because God knows, the thing known by God need
not exist.

If pain sometimes shatters the creature's false self-
sufficiency, yet in supreme " Trial " or " Sacrifice "
it teaches him the self-sufficiency which really ought
to be his—the " strength, which, if Heaven gave it,
may be called his own " : for then, in the absence of
all merely natural motives and supports, he acts in
that strength, and that alone, which God confers upon
him through his subjected will. Human will becomes
truly creative and truly our own when it is wholly
God's, and this is one of the many senses in which he
that loses his soul shall find it. In all other acts our
will is fed through nature, that is, through created
things other than the self—through the desires which
our physical organism and our heredity supply to us.
When we act from ourselves alone—that is, from
God *in* ourselves—we are collaborators in, or live
instruments of, creation : and that is why such an
act undoes with " backward mutters of dissevering
power " the uncreative spell which Adam laid upon
his species. Hence as suicide is the typical expression
of the stoic spirit, and battle of the warrior spirit,
martyrdom always remains the supreme enacting and
perfection of Christianity. This great action has
been initiated for us, done on our behalf, exemplified
for our imitation, and inconceivably communicated to
all believers, by Christ on Calvary. There the degree

of accepted Death reaches the utmost bounds of the
imaginable and perhaps goes beyond them ; not only
all natural supports, but the presence of the very
Father to whom the sacrifice is made deserts the
victim, and surrender to God does not falter though
God " forsakes " it.

The doctrine of death which I describe is not
peculiar to Christianity. Nature herself has written
it large across the world in the repeated drama of the
buried seed and the re-arising corn. From nature,
perhaps, the oldest agricultural communities learned
it and with animal, or human, sacrifices showed forth
for centuries the truth that " without shedding of
blood is no remission " [1] ; and though at first such
conceptions may have concerned only the crops and
offspring of the tribe they came later, in the Mysteries,
to concern the spiritual death and resurrection of the
individual. The Indian ascetic, mortifying his body
on a bed of spikes, preaches the same lesson ; the
Greek philosopher tells us that the life of wisdom is
" a practice of death ". [2] The sensitive and noble
heathen of modern times makes his imagined gods
" die into life ". [3]   Mr. Huxley expounds " non-
attachment ". We cannot escape the doctrine by
ceasing to be Christians. It is an " eternal gospel "
revealed to men wherever men have sought, or
endured, the truth : it is the very nerve of redemption, which anatomising wisdom at all times and in
all places lays bare; the unescapable knowledge which
the Light that lighteneth every man presses down

[1] Heb. ix, 22.
[2] Plato. Phæd., 81, A (cf. 64, A).
[3] Keats. Hyperion, III, 130.

upon the minds of all who seriously question what the universe is "about". The peculiarity of the Christian faith is not to teach this doctrine but to render it, in various ways, more tolerable. Christianity teaches us that the terrible task has already in some sense been accomplished for us—that a master's hand is holding ours as we attempt to trace the difficult letters and that our script need only be a "copy", not an original. Again, where other systems expose our total nature to death (as in Buddhist renunciation) Christianity demands only that we set right a *misdirection* of our nature, and has no quarrel, like Plato, with the body as such, nor with the psychical elements in our make-up. And sacrifice in its supreme realisation is not exacted of all. Confessors as well as martyrs are saved, and some old people whose state of grace we can hardly doubt seem to have got through their seventy years surprisingly easily. The sacrifice of Christ is repeated, or re-echoed, among His followers in very varying degrees, from the cruellest martyrdom down to a self-submission of intention whose outward signs have nothing to distinguish them from the ordinary fruits of temperance and "sweet reasonableness". The causes of this distribution I do not know; but from our present point of view it ought to be clear that the real problem is not why some humble, pious, believing people suffer, but why some do *not*. Our Lord Himself, it will be remembered, explained the salvation of those who are fortunate in this world only by referring to the unsearchable omnipotence of God.[1]

2 Mark x, 27.

All arguments in justification of suffering provoke bitter resentment against the author. You would like to know how I behave when I am experiencing pain, not writing books about it. You need not guess, for I will tell you; I am a great coward. But what is that to the purpose? When I think of pain—of anxiety that gnaws like fire and loneliness that spreads out like a desert, and the heartbreaking routine of monotonous misery, or again of dull aches that blacken our whole landscape or sudden nauseating pains that knock a man's heart out at one blow, of pains that seem already intolerable and then are suddenly increased, of infuriating scorpion-stinging pains that startle into maniacal movement a man who seemed half dead with his previous tortures—it " quite o'ercrows my spirit ". If I knew any way of escape I would crawl through sewers to find it. But what is the good of telling you about my feelings? You know them already : they are the same as yours. I am not arguing that pain is not painful. Pain hurts. That is what the word means. I am only trying to show that the old Christian doctrine of being made " perfect through suffering " [1] is not incredible. To prove it palatable is beyond my design.

In estimating the credibility of the doctrine two principles ought to be observed. In the first place we must remember that the actual moment of present pain is only the centre of what may be called the whole tribulational system which extends itself by fear and pity. Whatever good effects these experiences have are dependent upon the centre ; so that even if pain itself was of no spiritual value, yet, if fear and pity

[1] Heb. ii, 10.

were, pain would have to exist in order that there should be something to be feared and pitied. And that fear and pity help us in our return to obedience and charity is not to be doubted. Everyone has experienced the effect of pity in making it easier for us to love the unlovely—that is, to love men not because they are in any way naturally agreeable to us but because they are our brethren. The beneficence of fear most of us have learned during the period of " crises " that led up to the present war. My own experience is something like this. I am progressing along the path of life in my ordinary contentedly fallen and godless condition, absorbed in a merry meeting with my friends for the morrow or a bit of work that tickles my vanity to-day, a holiday or a new book, when suddenly a stab of abdominal pain that threatens serious disease, or a headline in the news-papers that threatens us all with destruction, sends this whole pack of cards tumbling down. At first I am overwhelmed, and all my little happinesses look like broken toys. Then, slowly and reluctantly, bit by bit, I try to bring myself into the frame of mind that I should be in at all times. I remind myself that all these toys were never intended to possess my heart, that my true good is in another world and my only real treasure is Christ. And perhaps, by God's grace, I succeed, and for a day or two become a creature consciously dependent on God and drawing its strength from the right sources. But the moment the threat is withdrawn, my whole nature leaps back to the toys : I am even anxious, God forgive me, to banish from my mind the only thing that supported me under the threat because it is now associated

with the misery of those few days. Thus the terrible
necessity of tribulation is only too clear. God has
had me for but forty-eight hours and then only by
dint of taking everything else away from me. Let
Him but sheathe that sword for a moment and I
behave like a puppy when the hated bath is over—I
shake myself as dry as I can and race off to reacquire
my comfortable dirtiness, if not in the nearest manure
heap, at least in the nearest flower bed. And that is
why tribulations cannot cease until God either
sees us remade or sees that our remaking is now
hopeless.

In the second place, when we are considering pain
itself—the centre of the whole tribulational system—
we must be careful to attend to what we know and
not to what we imagine. That is one of the reasons
why the whole central part of this book is devoted to
human pain, and animal pain is relegated to a special
chapter. About human pain we know, about animal
pain we only speculate. But even within the human
race we must draw our evidence from instances that
have come under our own observation. The
tendency of this or that novelist or poet may represent
suffering as wholly bad in its effects, as producing,
and justifying, every kind of malice and brutality in
the sufferer. And, of course, pain, like pleasure, can
be so received : all that is given to a creature with
free will must be two-edged, not by the nature of
the giver or of the gift, but by the nature of the
recipient.[1] And, again, the evil results of pain can be
multiplied if sufferers are persistently taught by the
bystanders that such results are the proper and manly

[1] On the two-edged nature of pain, see Appendix.

results for them to exhibit. Indignation at other's sufferings, though a generous passion, needs to be well managed lest it steal away patience and humility from those who suffer and plant anger and cynicism in their stead. But I am not convinced that suffering, if spared such officious vicarious indignation, has any natural tendency to produce such evils. I did not find the front-line trenches or the C.C.S. more full than any other place of hatred, selfishness, rebellion, and dishonesty. I have seen great beauty of spirit in some who were great sufferers. I have seen men, for the most part, grow better not worse with advancing years, and I have seen the last illness produce treasures of fortitude and meekness from most unpromising subjects. I see in loved and revered historical figures, such as Johnson and Cowper, traits which might scarcely have been tolerable if the men had been happier. If the world is indeed a "vale of soul making" it seems on the whole to be doing its work. Of poverty—the affliction which actually or potentially includes all other afflictions—I would not dare to speak as from myself; and those who reject Christianity will not be moved by Christ's statement that poverty is blessed. But here a rather remarkable fact comes to my aid. Those who would most scornfully repudiate Christianity as a mere "opiate of the people" have a contempt for the rich, that is, for all mankind *except* the poor. They regard the poor as the only people worth preserving from "liquidation", and place in them the only hope of the human race. But this is not compatible with a belief that the effects of poverty on those who suffer it are wholly evil; it even implies that they are good.

The Marxist thus finds himself in real agreement with the Christian in those two beliefs which Christianity paradoxically demands—that poverty is blessed and yet ought to be removed.

VII. HUMAN PAIN, *continued*

All things which are as they ought to be are conformed unto
this second law eternal; and even those things which to this
eternal law are not conformable are notwithstanding in some
sort ordered by *the first eternal law.*

HOOKER. *Laws of Eccles. Pol.*, I, iii, 1.

IN this chapter I advance six propositions necessary
to complete our account of human suffering which
do not arise out of one another and must therefore be
given in an arbitrary order.

1. There is a paradox about tribulation in Christianity. Blessed are the poor, but by " judgement "
(*i.e.*, social justice) and alms we are to remove poverty
wherever possible. Blessed are we when persecuted,
but we may avoid persecution by flying from city
to city, and may pray to be spared it, as Our Lord
prayed in Gethsemane. But if suffering is good,
ought it not to be pursued rather than avoided? I
answer that suffering is not good in itself. What is
good in any painful experience is, for the sufferer, his
submission to the will of God, and, for the spectators,
the compassion aroused and the acts of mercy to
which it leads. In the fallen and partially redeemed
universe we may distinguish (1) The simple good
descending from God, (2) The simple evil produced
by rebellious creatures, and (3) the exploitation of
that evil by God for His redemptive purpose, which
produces (4) the complex good to which accepted

suffering and repented sin contribute. Now the fact that God can make complex good out of simple evil does not excuse—though by mercy it may save— those who do the simple evil. And this distinction is central. Offences must come, but woe to those by whom they come ; sins *do* cause grace to abound, but we must not make that an excuse for continuing to sin. The crucifixion itself is the best, as well as the worst, of all historical events, but the *rôle* of Judas remains simply evil. We may apply this first to the problem of other people's suffering. A merciful man aims at his neighbour's good and so does " God's will ", consciously co-operating with " the simple good ". A cruel man oppresses his neighbour, and so does simple evil. But in doing such evil, he is used by God, without his own knowledge or consent, to produce the complex good—so that the first man serves God as a son, and the second as a tool. For you will certainly carry out God's purpose, however you act, but it makes a difference to you whether you serve like Judas or like John. The whole system is, so to speak, calculated for the clash between good men and bad men, and the good fruits of fortitude, patience, pity and forgiveness for which the cruel man is permitted to be cruel, presuppose that the good man ordinarily continues to seek simple good. I say " ordinarily " because a man is sometimes entitled to hurt (or even, in my opinion, to kill) his fellow, but only where the necessity is urgent and the good to be attained obvious, and usually (though not always) when he who inflicts the pain has a definite authority to do so—a parent's authority derived from nature, a magistrate's or soldier's derived from civil society, or a surgeon's derived, most often, from the patient. To turn this into a general charter for afflicting humanity " because affliction is good for them " (as Marlowe's lunatic Tamberlaine boasted himself the " scourge of God ") is not indeed to break the divine scheme but to volunteer for the post of Satan within that scheme. If you do his work, you must be prepared for his wages.

The problem about avoiding our own pain admits a similar solution. Some ascetics have used self-torture. As a layman, I offer no opinion on the prudence of such a regimen ; but I insist that, whatever its merits, self-torture is quite a different thing from tribulation sent by God. Everyone knows that fasting is a different experience from missing your dinner by accident or through poverty. Fasting asserts the will against the appetite—the reward being self-mastery and the danger pride : involuntary hunger subjects appetites and will together to the Divine will, furnishing an occasion for submission and exposing us to the danger of rebellion. But the redemptive effect of suffering lies chiefly in its tendency to reduce the rebel will. Ascetic practices, which in themselves strengthen the will, are only useful in so far as they enable the will to put its own house (the passions) in order, as a preparation for offering the whole man to God. They are necessary as a means ; as an end, they would be abominable, for in substituting will for appetite and there stopping, they would merely exchange the animal self for the diabolical self. It was, therefore, truly said that " only God can mortify ". Tribulation does its work in a world where human beings are ordinarily seeking,

by lawful means, to avoid their own natural evil and
to attain their natural good, and presupposes such a
world. In order to submit the will to God, we must
have a will and that will must have objects. Christian
renunciation does not mean stoic " Apathy ", but a
readiness to prefer God to inferior ends which are in
themselves lawful. Hence the Perfect Man brought
to Gethsemane a will, and a strong will, to escape
suffering and death if such escape were compatible
with the Father's will, combined with a perfect
readiness for obedience if it were not. Some of the
saints recommend a " total renunciation " at the very
threshold of our discipleship; but I think this can
mean only a total readiness for every particular
renunciation [1] that may be demanded, for it would
not be possible to live from moment to moment
willing nothing but submission to God as such.
What would be the *material* for the submission ? It
would seem self-contradictory to say " What I will is
to subject what I will to God's will ", for the second
what has no content. Doubtless we all spend too
much care in the avoidance of our own pain : but a
duly subordinated intention to avoid it, using lawful
means, is in accordance with " nature "—that is, with
the whole working system of creaturely life for which
the redemptive work of tribulation is calculated.

It would be quite false, therefore, to suppose that
the Christian view of suffering is incompatible with
the strongest emphasis on our duty to leave the world,
even in a temporal sense, " better " than we found it.

[1] *Cf.* Brother Lawrence, *Practice of the Presence of God*, IVth conversation, November 25th, 1667. The " one hearty renunciation " there is
" of everything which we are sensible does not lead us to God ".

In the fullest parabolic picture which He gave of the Judgement, Our Lord seems to reduce all virtue to active beneficence : and though it would be misleading to take that one picture in isolation from the Gospel as a whole, it is sufficient to place beyond doubt the basic principles of the social ethics of Christianity.

2. If tribulation is a necessary element in redemption, we must anticipate that it will never cease till God sees the world to be either redeemed or no further redeemable.   A Christian cannot, therefore, believe any of those who promise that if only some reform in our economic, political, or hygienic system were made, a heaven on earth would follow.   This might seem to have a discouraging effect on the social worker, but it is not found in practice to discourage him.   On the contrary, a strong sense of our common miseries, simply as men, is at least as good a spur to the removal of all the miseries we can, as any of those wild hopes which tempt men to seek their realisation by breaking the moral law and prove such dust and ashes when they are realised.   If applied to individual life, the doctrine that an imagined heaven on earth is necessary for vigorous attempts to remove present evil, would at once reveal its absurdity. Hungry men seek food and sick men healing none the less because they know that after the meal or the cure the ordinary ups and downs of life still await them. I am not, of course, discussing whether very drastic changes in our social system are, or are not, desirable ; I am only reminding the reader that a particular medicine is not to be mistaken for the elixir of life.

3. Since political issues have here crossed our path, I must make it clear that the Christian doctrine of

self-surrender and obedience is a purely theological, and not in the least a political, doctrine. Of forms of government, of civil authority and civil obedience, I have nothing to say. The kind and degree of obedience which a creature owes to its Creator is unique because the relation between creature and Creator is unique : no inference can be drawn from it to any political proposition whatsoever.

4. The Christian doctrine of suffering explains, I believe, a very curious fact about the world we live in. The settled happiness and security which we all desire, God withholds from us by the very nature of the world : but joy, pleasure, and merriment, He has scattered broadcast. We are never safe, but we have plenty of fun, and some ecstasy. It is not hard to see why. The security we crave would teach us to rest our hearts in this world and oppose an obstacle to our return to God : a few moments of happy love, a landscape, a symphony, a merry meeting with our friends, a bathe or a football match, have no such tendency. Our Father refreshes us on the journey with some pleasant inns, but will not encourage us to mistake them for home.

5. We must never make the problem of pain worse than it is by vague talk about the " unimaginable sum of human misery ". Suppose that I have a toothache of intensity x : and suppose that you, who are seated beside me, also begin to have a toothache of intensity x. You may, if you choose, say that the total amount of pain in the room is now $2x$. But you must remember that no one is suffering $2x$: search all time and all space and you will not find that composite pain in anyone's consciousness. There is no such

thing as a sum of suffering, for no one suffers it.
When we have reached the maximum that a single
person can suffer, we have, no doubt, reached something very horrible, but we have reached all the
suffering there ever can be in the universe. The
addition of a million fellow-sufferers adds no more
pain.

6. Of all evils, pain only is sterilised or disinfected
evil. Intellectual evil, or error, may recur because
the cause of the first error (such as fatigue or bad
handwriting) continues to operate : but quite apart
from that, error in its own right breeds error—if the
first step in an argument is wrong, everything that
follows will be wrong. Sin may recur because the
original temptation continues ; but quite apart from
that, sin of its very nature breeds sin by strengthening
sinful habit and weakening the conscience. Now
pain, like the other evils, may of course recur because
the cause of the first pain (disease, or an enemy) is
still operative : but pain has no tendency, in its own
right, to proliferate. When it is over, it is over, and
the natural sequel is joy. This distinction may be put
the other way round. After an error you need not
only to remove the causes (the fatigue or bad writing)
but also to correct the error itself : after a sin you
must not only, if possible, remove the temptation, you
must also go back and repent the sin itself. In each
case an " undoing " is required. Pain requires no
such undoing. You may need to heal the disease
which caused it, but the pain, once over, is sterile—
whereas every uncorrected error and unrepented sin
is, in its own right, a fountain of fresh error and fresh
sin flowing on to the end of time. Again, when I

err, my error infects every one who believes me. When I sin publicly, every spectator either condones it, thus sharing my guilt, or condemns it with imminent danger to his charity and humility. But suffering naturally produces in the spectators (unless they are unusually depraved) no bad effect, but a good one—pity. Thus that evil which God chiefly uses to produce the "complex good" is most markedly disinfected, or deprived of that proliferous tendency which is the worst characteristic of evil in general.

VIII. HELL

What is the world, O soldiers?
  It is I:
I, this incessant snow,
  This northern sky;
Soldiers, this solitude
  Through which we go
    Is I.

                    W. DE LA MARE. *Napoleon.*

Richard loves Richard; that is, I am I.
                              SHAKESPEARE.

IN an earlier chapter it was admitted that the pain
which alone could rouse the bad man to a knowledge
that all was not well, might also lead to a final and
unrepented rebellion. And it has been admitted
throughout that man has free will and that all gifts
to him are therefore two edged. From these premises
it follows directly that the Divine labour to redeem
the world cannot be certain of succeeding as regards
every individual soul. Some will not be redeemed.
There is no doctrine which I would more willingly
remove from Christianity than this, if it lay in my
power. But it has the full support of Scripture and,
specially, of Our Lord's own words; it has always
been held by Christendom; and it has the support of
reason. If a game is played, it must be possible to
lose it. If the happiness of a creature lies in self-
surrender, no one can make that surrender but

himself (though many can help him to make it) and he may refuse. I would pay any price to be able to say truthfully " All will be saved ". But my reason retorts, " Without their will, or with it ? " If I say " Without their will " I at once perceive a contradiction ; how can the supreme voluntary act of self-surrender be involuntary ? If I say " With their will ", my reason replies " How if they *will not* give in ? "

The Dominical utterances about Hell, like all Dominical sayings, are addressed to the conscience and the will, not to our intellectual curiosity. When they have roused us into action by convincing us of a terrible possibility, they have done, probably, all they were intended to do ; and if all the world were convinced Christians it would be unnecessary to say a word more on the subject. As things are, however, this doctrine is one of the chief grounds on which Christianity is attacked as barbarous, and the goodness of God impugned. We are told that it is a detestable doctrine—and indeed, I too detest it from the bottom of my heart—and are reminded of the tragedies in human life which have come from believing it. Of the other tragedies which come from not believing it we are told less. For these reasons, and these alone, it becomes necessary to discuss the matter.

The problem is not simply that of a God who consigns some of His creatures to final ruin. That would be the problem if we were Mahometans. Christianity, true, as always, to the complexity of the real, presents us with something knottier and more ambiguous—a God so full of mercy that He becomes

man and dies by torture to avert that final ruin from
His creatures, and who yet, where that heroic remedy
fails, seems unwilling, or even unable, to arrest the
ruin by an act of mere power. I said glibly a moment
ago that I would pay "any price" to remove this
doctrine. I lied. I could not pay one-thousandth
part of the price that God has already paid to remove
the *fact*. And here is the real problem: so much
mercy, yet still there is Hell.

I am not going to try to prove the doctrine
tolerable. Let us make no mistake; it is *not* tolerable.
But I think the doctrine can be shown to be moral,
by a critique of the objections ordinarily made, or
felt, against it.

First, there is an objection, in many minds, to the
idea of retributive punishment as such. This has
been partly dealt with in a previous chapter. It was
there maintained that all punishment became unjust
if the ideas of ill-desert and retribution were removed
from it; and a core of righteousness was discovered
within the vindictive passion itself, in the demand
that the evil man must not be left perfectly satisfied
with his own evil, that it must be made to appear to
him what it rightly appears to others—evil. I said
that Pain plants the flag of truth within a rebel
fortress. We were then discussing pain which might
still lead to repentance. How if it does not—if no
further conquest than the planting of the flag ever
takes place? Let us try to be honest with ourselves.
Picture to yourself a man who has risen to wealth or
power by a continued course of treachery and cruelty,
by exploiting for purely selfish ends the noble
motions of his victims, laughing the while at their

simplicity; who, having thus attained success, uses it for the gratification of lust and hatred and finally parts with the last rag of honour among thieves by betraying his own accomplices and jeering at their last moments of bewildered disillusionment. Suppose, further, that he does all this, not (as we like to imagine) tormented by remorse or even misgiving, but eating like a schoolboy and sleeping like a healthy infant—a jolly, ruddy-cheeked man, without a care in the world, unshakably confident to the very end that he alone has found the answer to the riddle of life, that God and man are fools whom he has got the better of, that his way of life is utterly successful, satisfactory, unassailable. We must be careful at this point. The least indulgence of the passion for revenge is very deadly sin. Christian charity counsels us to make every effort for the conversion of such a man : to prefer his conversion, at the peril of our own lives, perhaps of our own souls, to his punishment ; to prefer it infinitely. But that is not the question. Supposing he *will* not be converted, what destiny in the eternal world can you regard as proper for him ? Can you really desire that such a man, *remaining what he is* (and he must be able to do that if he has free will) should be confirmed forever in his present happiness—should continue, for all eternity, to be perfectly convinced that the laugh is on his side ? And if you cannot regard this as tolerable, is it only your wickedness—only spite—that prevents you from doing so ? Or do you find that conflict between Justice and Mercy, which has sometimes seemed to you such an outmoded piece of theology, now actually at work in your own mind, and feeling very much as if it came to you from above, not from below? You are moved not by a desire for the wretched creature's pain as such, but by a truly ethical demand that, soon or late, the right should be asserted, the flag planted in this horribly rebellious soul, even if no fuller and better conquest is to follow. In a sense, it is better for the creature itself, even if it never becomes good, that it should know itself a failure, a mistake. Even mercy can hardly wish to such a man his eternal, contented continuance in such ghastly illusion. Thomas Aquinas said of suffering, as Aristotle had said of shame, that it was a thing not good in itself, but a thing which might have a certain goodness in particular circumstances. That is to say, if evil is present, pain at recognition of the evil, being a kind of knowledge, is relatively good; for the alternative is that the soul should be ignorant of the evil, or ignorant that the evil is contrary to its nature, "either of which", says the philosopher, "is *manifestly* bad".[1]   And I think, though we tremble, we agree.

The demand that God should forgive such a man while he remains what he is, is based on a confusion between condoning and forgiving. To condone an evil is simply to ignore it, to treat it as if it were good. But forgiveness needs to be accepted as well as offered if it is to be complete : and a man who admits no guilt can accept no forgiveness.

I have begun with the conception of Hell as a positive retributive punishment inflicted by God because that is the form in which the doctrine is most repellent, and I wished to tackle the strongest objec-

[1] *Summa Theol.*, I, II^{ae}, Q. xxxix, Art. 1.

tion. But, of course, though Our Lord often speaks
of Hell as a sentence inflicted by a tribunal, He also
says elsewhere that the judgement consists in the very
fact that men prefer darkness to light, and that not
He, but His " word ", judges men.[1] We are therefore
at liberty—since the two conceptions, in the long
run, mean the same thing—to think of this bad man's
perdition not as a sentence imposed on him but as the
mere fact of being what he is. The characteristic of
lost souls is " their rejection of everything that is
not simply themselves ".[2] Our imaginary egoist has
tried to turn everything he meets into a province or
appendage of the self. The taste for the *other*, that is,
the very capacity for enjoying good, is quenched in
him except in so far as his body still draws him into
some rudimentary contact with an outer world.
Death removes this last contact. He has his wish—
to live wholly in the self and to make the best of what
he finds there. And what he finds there is Hell.

Another objection turns on the apparent dispropor-
tion between eternal damnation and transitory sin.
And if we think of eternity as a mere prolongation of
time, it is disproportionate. But many would reject
this idea of eternity. If we think of time as a line—
which is a good image, because the parts of time are
successive and no two of them can co-exist ; *i.e.*,
there is no *width* in time, only length—we probably
ought to think of eternity as a plane or even a solid.
Thus the whole reality of a human being would be
represented by a solid figure. That solid would be

[1] John iii, 19 ; xii, 48.
[2] See von Hügel, Essays and Addresses, 1st series, *What do we mean
by Heaven and Hell?*

mainly the work of God, acting through grace and nature, but human free will would have contributed the base-line which we call earthly life : and if you draw your base line askew, the whole solid will be in the wrong place. The fact that life is short, or, in the symbol, that we contribute only one little line to the whole complex figure, might be regarded as a Divine mercy. For if even the drawing of that little line, left to our free will, is sometimes so badly done as to spoil the whole, how much worse a mess might we have made of the figure if more had been entrusted to us ? A simpler form of the same objection consists in saying that death ought not to be final, that there ought to be a second chance.[1] I believe that if a million chances were likely to do good, they would be given. But a master often knows, when boys and parents do not, that it is really useless to send a boy in for a certain examination again. Finality must come some time, and it does not require a very robust faith to believe that omniscience knows when.

A third objection turns on the frightful intensity of the pains of Hell as suggested by mediæval art and, indeed, by certain passages in Scripture. Von Hügel here warns us not to confuse the doctrine itself with the *imagery* by which it may be conveyed. Our Lord speaks of Hell under three symbols : first, that of punishment ("everlasting punishment," Matt. xxv, 46) ; second, that of destruction ("fear Him who is able to destroy both body and soul in Hell," Matt. x, 28) ; and thirdly, that of privation, exclusion, or

---

[1] The conception of a "second chance" must not be confused either with that of Purgatory (for souls already saved) or of Limbo (for souls already lost).

banishment into " the darkness outside ", as in the
parables of the man without a wedding garment or of
the wise and foolish virgins. The prevalent image of
fire is significant because it combines the ideas of
torment and destruction. Now it is quite certain
that all these expressions are intended to suggest
something unspeakably horrible, and any interpretation which does not face that fact is, I am afraid, out
of court from the beginning. But it is not necessary
to concentrate on the images of torture to the exclusion
of those suggesting destruction and privation. What
can that be whereof all three images are equally
proper symbols ? Destruction, we should naturally
assume, means the unmaking, or cessation, of the
destroyed. And people often talk as if the " annihila-
tion " of a soul were intrinsically possible. In all our
experience, however, the destruction of one thing
means the emergence of something else. Burn a log,
and you have gases, heat and ash. To *have been* a log
means now being those three things. If soul can be
destroyed, must there not be a state of *having been* a
human soul ? And is not that, perhaps, the state
which is equally well described as torment, destruction, and privation ? You will remember that in the
parable, the saved go to a place prepared for *them*,
while the damned go to a place never made for men
at all.[1] To enter heaven is to become more human
than you ever succeeded in being in earth ; to enter
hell, is to be banished from humanity. What is cast
(or casts itself) into hell is not a man : it is " remains ".
To be a complete man means to have the passions
obedient to the will and the will offered to God : to

[1] Matt. xxv, 34, 41.

have been a man—to be an ex-man or "damned ghost"—would presumably mean to consist of a will utterly centred in its self and passions utterly uncontrolled by the will. It is, of course, impossible to imagine what the consciousness of such a creature— already a loose congeries of mutually antagonistic sins rather than a sinner—would be like. There may be a truth in the saying that "hell is hell, not from its own point of view, but from the heavenly point of view". I do not think this belies the severity of Our Lord's words. It is only to the damned that their fate could ever seem less than unendurable. And it must be admitted that as, in these last chapters, we think of eternity, the categories of pain and pleasure, which have engaged us so long, begin to recede, as vaster good and evil looms in sight. Neither pain nor pleasure as such has the last word. Even if it were possible that the experience (if it can be called experience) of the lost contained no pain and much pleasure, still, that black pleasure would be such as to send any soul, not already damned, flying to its prayers in nightmare terror: even if there were pains in heaven, all who understand would desire them.

A fourth objection is that no charitable man could himself be blessed in heaven while he knew that even one human soul was still in hell; and if so, are we more merciful than God? At the back of this objection lies a mental picture of heaven and hell co-existing in unilinear time as the histories of England and America co-exist: so that at each moment the blessed could say "The miseries of hell are *now* going on". But I notice that Our Lord,

while stressing the terror of hell with unsparing
severity usually emphasises the idea not of duration
but of *finality*. Consignment to the destroying fire
is usually treated as the end of the story—not as the
beginning of a new story. That the lost soul is
eternally fixed in its diabolical attitude we cannot
doubt : but whether this eternal fixity implies endless
duration—or duration at all—we cannot say. Dr.
Edwyn Bevan has some interesting speculations on
this point.[1] We know much more about heaven than
hell, for heaven is the home of humanity and therefore
contains all that is implied in a glorified human life :
but hell was not made for men. It is in no sense
parallel to heaven : it is " the darkness outside ",
the outer rim where being fades away into nonentity.

Finally, it is objected that the ultimate loss of a
single soul means the defeat of omnipotence. And so
it does. In creating beings with free will, omnipotence
from the outset submits to the possibility of such
defeat. What you call defeat, I call miracle : for to
make things which are not Itself, and thus to become,
in a sense, capable of being resisted by its own
handiwork, is the most astonishing and unimaginable
of all the feats we attribute to the Deity. I willingly
believe that the damned are, in one sense, successful,
rebels to the end ; that the doors of hell are locked on
the *inside*. I do not mean that the ghosts may not
wish to come out of hell, in the vague fashion wherein
an envious man " wishes " to be happy : but they
certainly do not will even the first preliminary stages
of that self-abandonment through which alone the
soul can reach any good. They enjoy forever the

[1] *Symbolism and Belief*, p. 101.

horrible freedom they have demanded, and are
therefore self-enslaved : just as the blessed, forever
submitting to obedience, become through all eternity
more and more free.

In the long run the answer to all those who object
to the doctrine of hell, is itself a question : " What
are you asking God to do ? " To wipe out their past
sins and, at all costs, to give them a fresh start,
smoothing every difficulty and offering every
miraculous help ? But He has done so, on Calvary.
To forgive them ? They will not be forgiven. To
leave them alone ? Alas, I am afraid that is what He
does.

One caution, and I have done. In order to rouse
modern minds to an understanding of the issues, I
ventured to introduce in this chapter a picture of the
sort of bad man whom we most easily perceive to be
truly bad. But when the picture has done that work,
the sooner it is forgotten the better. In all discussions
of Hell we should keep steadily before our eyes the
possible damnation, not of our enemies nor our
friends (since both these disturb the reason) but of
ourselves. This chapter is not about your wife or
son, nor about Nero or Judas Iscariot ; it is about
you and me.

IX. ANIMAL PAIN

And whatsoever Adam called every living creature, that was the name thereof.

Genesis ii, 19.

To find out what is natural, we must study specimens which retain their nature and not those which have been corrupted.

ARISTOTLE. *Politics*, I, v, 5.

THUS far of human suffering; but all this time " a plaint of guiltless hurt doth pierce the sky ". The problem of animal suffering is appalling; not because the animals are so numerous (for, as we have seen, no more pain is felt when a million suffer than when one suffers) but because the Christian explanation of human pain cannot be extended to animal pain. So far as we know beasts are incapable either of sin or virtue : therefore they can neither deserve pain nor be improved by it. At the same time we must never allow the problem of animal suffering to become the centre of the problem of pain; not because it is unimportant—whatever furnishes plausible grounds for questioning the goodness of God is very important indeed—but because it is outside the range of our knowledge. God has given us data which enable us, in some degree, to understand our own suffering : He has given us no such data about beasts. We know neither why they were made nor what they are, and everything we say about them is speculative. From

the doctrine that God is good we may confidently
deduce that the *appearance* of reckless divine cruelty
in the animal kingdom is an illusion—and the fact
that the only suffering we know at first hand (our
own) turns out not to be a cruelty will make it easier
to believe this. After that, everything is guesswork.

We may begin by ruling out some of the pessimistic
bluff put up in the first chapter. The fact that
vegetable lives " prey upon " one another and are in
a state of " ruthless " competition is of no moral
importance at all. " Life " in the biological sense has
nothing to do with good and evil until sentience
appears. The very words " prey " and " ruthless "
are mere metaphors. Wordsworth believed that
every flower " enjoyed the air it breathes ", but there
is no reason to suppose he was right. No doubt,
living plants react to injuries differently from inorganic
matter ; but an anæsthetised human body reacts more
differently still and such reactions do not prove
sentience. We are, of course, justified in speaking of
the death or thwarting of a plant as if it were a
tragedy, provided that we know we are using a
metaphor. To furnish symbols for spiritual experiences may be one of the functions of the mineral and
vegetable worlds. But we must not become the
victims of our metaphor. A forest in which half the
trees are killing the other half may be a perfectly
" good " forest : for its goodness consists in its
utility and beauty and it does not feel.

When we turn to the beasts, three questions arise.
There is, first, the question of fact ; what do animals
suffer ? There is, secondly, the question of origin ;
how did disease and pain enter the animal world ?

And, thirdly, there is the question of justice; how can animal suffering be reconciled with the justice of God?

1. In the long run the answer to the first question is, We don't know; but some speculations may be worth setting down. We must begin by distinguishing among animals: for if the ape could understand us he would take it very ill to be lumped along with the oyster and the earth-worm in a single class of " animals " and contrasted to men. Clearly in some ways the ape and man are much more like each other than either is like the worm. At the lower end of the animal realm we need not assume anything we could recognise as sentience. Biologists in distinguishing animal from vegetable do not make use of sentience or locomotion or other such characteristics as a layman would naturally fix upon. At some point, however (though where, we cannot say), sentience almost certainly comes in, for the higher animals have nervous systems very like our own. But at this level we must still distinguish sentience from consciousness. If you happen never to have heard of this distinction before, I am afraid you will find it rather startling, but it has great authority and you would be ill-advised to dismiss it out of hand. Suppose that three sensations follow one another—first A, then B, then C. When this happens to you, you have the experience of passing through the process ABC. But note what this implies. It implies that there is something in you which stands sufficiently outside A to notice A passing away, and sufficiently outside B to notice B now beginning and coming to fill the place which A has vacated; and something which recognises itself

as the same through the transition from A to B and B to C, so that it can say "I have had the experience ABC." Now this something is what I call Consciousness or Soul and the process I have just described is one of the proofs that the soul, though experiencing time, is not itself completely "timeful". The simplest experience of ABC as a succession demands a soul which is not itself a mere succession of states, but rather a permanent bed along which these different portions of the stream of sensation roll, and which recognises itself as the same beneath them all. Now it is almost certain that the nervous system of one of the higher animals presents it with successive sensations. It does not follow that it has any "soul", anything which recognises itself as having had A, and now having B, and now marking how B glides away to make room for C. If it had no such "soul", what we call the experience ABC would never occur. There would, in philosophic language, be "a succession of perceptions"; that is, the sensations would, in fact, occur in that order, and God would know that they were so occurring, but the animal would not know. There would not be "a perception of succession". This would mean that if you give such a creature two blows with a whip, there are, indeed, two pains: but there is no co-ordinating self which can recognise that "I have had two pains". Even in the single pain, there is no self to say "I am in pain"—for if it could distinguish itself from the sensation—the bed from the stream—sufficiently to say "I am in pain" it would also be able to connect the two sensations as *its* experience. The correct description would be "Pain is taking place in this animal "; not, as we commonly say, " This animal feels pain ", for the words " this " and " feels " really smuggle in the assumption that it is a " self " or " soul " or " consciousness " standing above the sensations and organising them into an " experience " as we do. Such sentience without consciousness, I admit, we cannot imagine : not because it never occurs in us, but because, when it does, we describe ourselves as being " unconscious ". And rightly. The fact that animals react to pain much as we do is, of course, no proof that they are conscious ; for we may also so react under chloroform, and even answer questions while asleep.

How far up the scale such unconscious sentience may extend, I will not even guess. It is certainly difficult to suppose that the apes, the elephant, and the higher domestic animals, have not, in some degree, a self or soul which connects experiences and gives rise to rudimentary individuality. But at least a great deal of what appears to be animal suffering need not be suffering in any real sense. It may be we who have invented the " sufferers " by the " pathetic fallacy " of reading into the beats a self for which there is no real evidence.

2. The origin of animal suffering could be traced, by earlier generations, to the Fall of man—the whole world was infected by the uncreating rebellion of Adam. This is now impossible, for we have good reason to believe that animals existed long before men. Carnivorousness, with all that it entails, is older than humanity. Now it is impossible at this point not to remember a certain sacred story which, though never included in the creeds, has been widely believed in

the Church and seems to be implied in several
Dominical, Pauline, and Johannine utterances—I
mean the story that man was not the first creature to
rebel against the Creator, but that some older and
mightier being long since became apostate and is now
the emperor of darkness and (significantly) the Lord
of this world. Some people would like to reject all
such elements from Our Lord's teaching: and it
might be argued that when He emptied Himself of
His glory He also humbled Himself to share, as man,
the current superstitions of His time. And I certainly
think that Christ, in the flesh, was not omniscient—if
only because a human brain could not, presumably,
be the vehicle of omniscient consciousness, and to
say that Our Lord's thinking was not really condi-
tioned by the size and shape of His brain might be
to deny the real incarnation and become a Docetist.
Thus, if Our Lord had committed Himself to any
scientific or historical statement which we knew to be
untrue, this would not disturb my faith in His deity.
But the doctrine of Satan's existence and fall is not
among the things we know to be untrue: it contra-
dicts not the facts discovered by scientists but the
mere, vague " climate of opinion " that we happen
to be living in. Now I take a very low view of
" climates of opinion ". In his own subject every
man knows that all discoveries are made and all
errors corrected by those who ignore the " climate of
opinion ".

It seems to me, therefore, a reasonable supposition,
that some mighty created power had already been at
work for ill on the material universe, or the solar
system, or, at least, the planet Earth, before ever man

came on the scene : and that when man fell, someone had, indeed, tempted him. This hypothesis is not introduced as a general " explanation of evil " : it only gives a wider application to the principle that evil comes from the abuse of free-will. If there is such a power, as I myself believe, it may well have corrupted the animal creation before man appeared. The intrinsic evil of the animal world lies in the fact that animals, or some animals, live by destroying each other. That plants do the same I will not admit to be an evil. The Satanic corruption of the beasts would therefore be analogous, in one respect, with the Satanic corruption of man. For one result of man's fall was that his animality fell back from the humanity into which it had been taken up but which could no longer rule it. In the same way, animality may have been encouraged to slip back into behaviour proper to vegetables. It is, of course, true that the immense mortality occasioned by the fact that many beasts live on beasts is balanced, in nature, by an immense birth-rate, and it might seem, that if all animals had been herbivorous and healthy, they would mostly starve as a result of their own multiplication. But I take the fecundity and the death-rate to be correlative phenomena. There was, perhaps, no necessity for such an excess of the sexual impulse : the Lord of this world thought of it as a response to carnivorousness—a double scheme for securing the maximum amount of torture. If it offends less, you may say that the " life-force " is corrupted, where I say that living creatures were corrupted by an evil angelic being. We mean the same thing : but I find it easier to believe in a myth of gods and demons than in one of hypostatised abstract nouns. And after all, our mythology may be much nearer to literal truth than we suppose. Let us not forget that Our Lord, on one occasion, attributes human disease not to God's wrath, nor to nature, but quite explicitly to Satan.[1]

If this hypothesis is worth considering, it is also worth considering whether man, at his first coming into the world, had not already a redemptive function to perform. Man, even now, can do wonders to animals: my cat and dog live together in my house and seem to like it. It may have been one of man's functions to restore peace to the animal world, and if he had not joined the enemy he might have succeeded in doing so to an extent now hardly imaginable.

3. Finally, there is the question of justice. We have seen reason to believe that not all animals suffer as we think they do: but some, at least, look as if they had selves, and what shall be done for these innocents? And we have seen that it is possible to believe that animal pain is not God's handiwork but begun by Satan's malice and perpetuated by man's desertion of his post: still, if God has not caused it, He has permitted it, and, once again, what shall be done for these innocents? I have been warned not even to raise the question of animal immortality, lest I find myself " in company with all the old maids ".[2] I have no objection to the company. I do not think either virginity or old age contemptible, and some of the shrewdest minds I have met inhabited the bodies of old maids.[2] Nor am I greatly moved by jocular

[1] Luke xiii, 16.
[2] But also with J. Wesley, *Sermon LXV. The Great Deliverance.*

enquiries such as "Where will you put all the
mosquitoes?"—a question to be answered on its
own level by pointing out that, if the worst came to
the worst, a heaven for mosquitoes and a hell for men
could very conveniently be combined. The complete
silence of Scripture and Christian tradition on animal
immortality is a more serious objection; but it would
be fatal only if Christian revelation showed any signs
of being intended as a *système de la nature* answering
all questions. But it is nothing of the sort: the
curtain has been rent at one point, and at one point
only, to reveal our immediate practical necessities
and not to satisfy our intellectual curiosity. If
animals were, in fact, immortal, it is unlikely, from
what we discern of God's method in the revelation,
that He would have revealed this truth. Even our
own immortality is a doctrine that comes late in the
history of Judaism. The argument from silence is
therefore very weak.

The real difficulty about supposing most animals
to be immortal is that immortality has almost no
meaning for a creature which is not "conscious" in
the sense explained above. If the life of a newt is
merely a succession of sensations, what should we
mean by saying that God may recall to life the newt
that died to-day? It would not recognise itself as the
same newt; the pleasant sensations of any other newt
that lived after its death would be just as much, or
just as little, a recompense for its earthly sufferings
(if any) as those of its resurrected—I was going to
say "self", but the whole point is that the newt
probably has no self. The thing we have to try to
say, on this hypothesis, will not even be said. There

is, therefore, I take it, no question of immortality for creatures that are merely sentient. Nor do justice and mercy demand that there should be, for such creatures have no painful experience. Their nervous system delivers all the *letters* A, P, N, I, but since they cannot read they never build it up into the word PAIN. And all animals *may* be in that condition.

If, nevertheless, the strong conviction which we have of a real, though doubtless rudimentary, selfhood in the higher animals, and specially in those we tame, is not an illusion, their destiny demands a somewhat deeper consideration. The error we must avoid is that of considering them in themselves. Man is to be understood only in his relation to God. The beasts are to be understood only in their relation to man and, through man, to God. Let us here guard against one of those untransmuted lumps of atheistical thought which often survive in the minds of modern believers. Atheists naturally regard the co-existence of man and the other animals as a mere contingent result of interacting biological facts ; and the taming of an animal by a man as a purely arbitrary interference of one species with another. The " real " or " natural " animal to them is the wild one, and the tame animal is an artificial or unnatural thing. But a Christian must not think so. Man was appointed by God to have dominion over the beasts, and everything a man does to an animal is either a lawful exercise, or a sacrilegious abuse, of an authority by divine right. The tame animal is therefore, in the deepest sense, the only " natural " animal—the only one we see occupying the place it was made to occupy, and it is on the tame animal that we must base all our doctrine of

beasts. Now it will be seen that, in so far as the tame
animal has a real self or personality, it owes this
almost entirely to its master. If a good sheepdog
seems "almost human" that is because a good
shepherd has made it so. I have already noted the
mysterious force of the word "in". I do not take
all the senses of it in the New Testament to be
identical, so that man is *in* Christ and Christ *in* God
and the Holy Spirit *in* the Church and also *in* the
individual believer in exactly the same sense. They
may be senses that rhyme or correspond rather than
a single sense. I am now going to suggest—though
with great readiness to be set right by real theologians
—that there may be a sense, corresponding, though
not identical, with these, in which those beasts that
attain a real self are *in* their masters. That is to say,
you must not think of a beast by itself, and call that a
personality and then inquire whether God will raise
and bless *that*. You must take the whole context *in*
which the beast acquires its selfhood—namely "The-
goodman - and - the - goodwife - ruling - their -
children - and - their - beasts - in - the - good - homestead". That whole context may be regarded as a
"body" in the Pauline (or a closely sub-Pauline)
sense; and how much of that "body" may be raised
along with the goodman and the goodwife, who can
predict? So much, presumably, as is necessary not
only for the glory of God and the beatitude of the
human pair, but for that particular glory and that
particular beatitude which is eternally coloured by
that particular terrestrial experience. And in this way
it seems to me possible that certain animals may have
an immortality, not in themselves, but in the immor-

tality of their masters. And the difficulty about personal identity in a creature barely personal disappears when the creature is thus kept in its proper context. If you ask, concerning an animal thus raised as a member of the whole Body of the homestead, where its personal identity resides, I answer "Where its identity always did reside even in the earthly life—in its relation to the Body and, specially, to the master who is the head of that Body". In other words, the man will know his dog: the dog will know its master and, in knowing him, will *be* itself. To ask that it should, in any other way, *know* itself, is probably to ask for what has no meaning. Animals aren't like that, and don't want to be.

My picture of the good sheepdog in the good homestead does not, of course, cover wild animals nor (a matter even more urgent) ill-treated domestic animals. But it is intended only as an illustration drawn from one privileged instance—which is, also, on my view the only normal and unperverted instance —of the general principles to be observed in framing a theory of animal resurrection. I think Christians may justly hesitate to suppose any beasts immortal, for two reasons. Firstly, because they fear, by attributing to beasts a "soul" in the full sense, to obscure that difference between beast and man which is as sharp in the spiritual dimension as it is hazy and problematical in the biological. And secondly, a future happiness connected with the beast's present life simply as a compensation for suffering—so many millenniums in the happy pastures paid down as "damages" for so many years of pulling carts—

seems a clumsy assertion of Divine goodness. We, because we are fallible, often hurt a child or an animal unintentionally, and then the best we can do is to "make up for it" by some caress or tit-bit. But it is hardly pious to imagine omniscience acting in that way—as though God trod on the animals' tails in the dark and then did the best He could about it! In such a botched adjustment I cannot recognise the master-touch; whatever the answer is, it must be something better than that. The theory I am suggesting tries to avoid both objections. It makes God the centre of the universe and man the subordinate centre of terrestrial nature : the beasts are not co-ordinate with man, but subordinate to him, and their destiny is through and through related to his. And the derivative immortality suggested for them is not a mere *amende* or compensation : it is part and parcel of the new heaven and new earth, organically related to the whole suffering process of the world's fall and redemption.

Supposing, as I do, that the personality of the tame animals is largely the gift of man—that their mere sentience is reborn to soulhood in us as our mere soulhood is reborn to spirituality in Christ—I naturally suppose that very few animals indeed, in their wild state, attain to a "self" or *ego*. But if any do, and if it is agreeable to the goodness of God that they should live again, their immortality would also be related to man—not, this time, to individual masters, but to humanity. That is to say, if in any instance the quasi-spiritual and emotional value which human tradition attributes to a beast (such as the "innocence" of the lamb or the heraldic royalty of the lion) has a real ground in the beast's nature, and is not merely arbitrary or accidental, then it is in *that* capacity, or principally in that, that the beast may be expected to attend on risen man and make part of his " train ".   Or if the traditional character is quite erroneous, then the beast's heavenly life [1] would be in virtue of the real, but unknown, effect it has actually had on man during his whole history : for if Christian cosmology is in *any* sense (I do not say, in a literal sense) true, then all that exists on our planet is related to man, and even the creatures that were extinct before men existed are then only seen in their true light when they are seen as the unconscious harbingers of man.

When we are speaking of creatures so remote from us as wild beasts, and prehistoric beasts, we hardly know what we are talking about.   It may well be that they have no selves and no sufferings.   It may even be that each species has a corporate self—that Lionhood, not lions, has shared in the travail of creation and will enter into the restoration of all things.   And if we cannot imagine even our own eternal life, much less can we imagine the life the beasts may have as our " members ".   If the earthly lion could read the prophecy of that day when he shall eat hay like an ox, he would regard it as a description not of heaven, but of hell.   And if there is nothing in the lion but carnivorous sentience, then he is unconscious and his " survival " would have no meaning.   But if there is a rudimentary Leonine self, to that also God can give a " body " as it pleases

---

[1] That is, its participation in the heavenly life of men *in* Christ *to* God ; to suggest a " heavenly life " for the beast *as such* is probably nonsense.

Him—a body no longer living by the destruction of the lamb, yet richly Leonine in the sense that it also expresses whatever energy and splendour and exulting power dwelled within the visible lion on this earth. I think, under correction, that the prophet used an eastern hyperbole when he spoke of the lion and the lamb *lying down* together. That would be rather impertinent of the lamb. To have lions and lambs that so consorted (except on some rare celestial Saturnalia of topsy-turvydom) would be the same as having neither lambs nor lions. I think the lion, when he has ceased to be dangerous, will still be awful : indeed, that we shall then first see that of which the present fangs and claws are a clumsy, and satanically perverted, imitation. There will still be something like the shaking of a golden mane : and often the good Duke will say, " Let him roar again ".

X. HEAVEN

It is required
You do awake your faith. Then all stand still ;
On ; those that think it is unlawful business
I am about, let them depart.

SHAKESPEARE. *Winter's Tale.*

Plunged in thy depth of mercy let me die
The death that every soul that lives desires.

COWPER out of *Madame Guion.*

" I RECKON ", said St. Paul, " that the sufferings of
this present time are not worthy to be compared with
the glory that shall be revealed in us." [1] If this is so,
a book on suffering which says nothing of heaven, is
leaving out almost the whole of one side of the
account. Scripture and tradition habitually put the
joys of heaven into the scale against the sufferings of
earth, and no solution of the problem of pain which
does not do so can be called a Christian one. We are
very shy nowadays of even mentioning heaven. We
are afraid of the jeer about " pie in the sky ", and of
being told that we are trying to " escape " from the
duty of making a happy world here and now into
dreams of a happy world elsewhere. But either there
is " pie in the sky " or there is not. If there is not,
then Christianity is false, for this doctrine is woven

Rom. viii, 18.

into its whole fabric. If there is, then this truth, like any other, must be faced, whether it is useful at political meetings or no. Again, we are afraid that heaven is a bribe, and that if we make it our goal we shall no longer be disinterested. It is not so. Heaven offers nothing that a mercenary soul can desire. It is safe to tell the pure in heart that they shall see God, for only the pure in heart want to. There are rewards that do not sully motives. A man's love for a woman is not mercenary because he wants to marry her, nor his love for poetry mercenary because he wants to read it, nor his love of exercise less disinterested because he wants to run and leap and walk. Love, by definition, seeks to enjoy its object.

You may think that there is another reason for our silence about heaven—namely, that we do not really desire it. But that may be an illusion. What I am now going to say is merely an opinion of my own without the slightest authority, which I submit to the judgement of better Christians and better scholars than myself. There have been times when I think we do not desire heaven; but more often I find myself wondering whether, in our heart of hearts, we have ever desired anything else. You may have noticed that the books you really love are bound together by a secret thread. You know very well what is the common quality that makes you love them, though you cannot put it into words: but most of your friends do not see it at all, and often wonder why, liking this, you should also like that. Again, you have stood before some landscape, which seems to embody what you have been looking for all your life; and then turned to the friend at your side who appears to be seeing what you saw—but at the first words a gulf yawns between you, and you realise that this landscape means something totally different to him, that he is pursuing an alien vision and cares nothing for the ineffable suggestion by which you are transported. Even in your hobbies, has there not always been some secret attraction which the others are curiously ignorant of—something, not to be identified with, but always on the verge of breaking through, the smell of cut wood in the workshop or the clap-clap of water against the boat's side? Are not all lifelong friendships born at the moment when at last you meet another human being who has some inkling (but faint and uncertain even in the best) of that something which you were born desiring, and which, beneath the flux of other desires and in all the momentary silences between the louder passions, night and day, year by year, from childhood to old age, you are looking for, watching for, listening for? You have never *had* it. All the things that have ever deeply possessed your soul have been but hints of it—tantalising glimpses, promises never quite fulfilled, echoes that died away just as they caught your ear. But if it should really become manifest—if there ever came an echo that did not die away but swelled into the sound itself—you would know it. Beyond all possibility of doubt you would say " Here at last is the thing I was made for ". We cannot tell each other about it. It is the secret signature of each soul, the incommunicable and unappeasable want, the thing we desired before we met our wives or made our friends or chose our work, and which we shall still desire on our deathbeds, when the mind no longer

knows wife or friend or work. While we are, this is.
If we lose this, we lose all.[1]

This signature on each soul may be a product of
heredity and environment, but that only means that
heredity and environment are among the instruments
whereby God creates a soul. I am considering not
how, but why, He makes each soul unique. If He
had no use for all these differences, I do not see why
He should have created more souls than one. Be sure
that the ins and outs of your individuality are no
mystery to Him; and one day they will no longer be a
mystery to you. The mould in which a key is made
would be a strange thing, if you had never seen a key:
and the key itself a strange thing if you had never
seen a lock. Your soul has a curious shape because
it is a hollow made to fit a particular swelling in the
infinite contours of the divine substance, or a key to
unlock one of the doors in the house with many
mansions. For it is not humanity in the abstract
that is to be saved, but you—you, the individual
reader, John Stubbs or Janet Smith. Blessed and
fortunate creature, your eyes shall behold Him and
not another's. All that you are, sins apart, is destined,
if you will let God have His good way, to utter
satisfaction. The Brocken spectre " looked to every
man like his first love ", because she was a cheat.
But God will look to every soul like its first love
because He is its first love. Your place in heaven will
seem to be made for you and you alone, because you

---

[1] I am not, of course, suggesting that these immortal longings which
we have from the Creator because we are men, should be confused
with the gifts of the Holy Spirit to those who are in Christ. We must
not fancy we are holy because we are human.

were made for it—made for it stitch by stitch as a glove is made for a hand.

It is from this point of view that we can understand Hell in its aspect of privation. All your life an unattainable ecstasy has hovered just beyond the grasp of your consciousness. The day is coming when you will wake to find, beyond all hope, that you have attained it, or else, that it was within your reach and you have lost it forever.

This may seem a perilously private and subjective notion of the pearl of great price, but it is not. The thing I am speaking of is not an experience. You have experienced only the *want* of it. The thing itself has never actually been embodied in any thought, or image, or emotion. Always it has summoned you out of yourself. And if you will not go out of yourself to follow it, if you sit down to brood on the desire and attempt to cherish it, the desire itself will evade you. " The door into life generally opens behind us " and " the only wisdom " for one " haunted with the scent of unseen roses, is work." [1] This secret fire goes out when you use the bellows : bank it down with what seems unlikely fuel of dogma and ethics, turn your back on it and attend to your duties, and then it will blaze. The world is like a picture with a golden background, and we the figures in that picture. Until you step off the plane of the picture into the large dimensions of death you cannot see the gold. But we have reminders of it. To change our metaphor, the black-out is not quite complete. There are chinks. At times the daily scene looks big with its secret.

[1] George Macdonald. *Alec Forbes*, cap. XXXIII.

Such is my opinion; and it may be erroneous. Perhaps this secret desire also is part of the Old Man and must be crucified before the end. But this opinion has a curious trick of evading denial. The desire—much more the satisfaction—has always refused to be fully present in any experience. Whatever you try to identify with it, turns out to be not it but something else: so that hardly any degree of crucifixion or transformation could go beyond what the desire itself leads us to anticipate. Again, if this opinion is not true, something better is. But " something better "—not this or that experience, but beyond it—is almost the definition of the thing I am trying to describe.

The thing you long for summons you away from the self. Even the desire for the thing lives only if you abandon it. This is the ultimate law—the seed dies to live, the bread must be cast upon the waters, he that loses his soul will save it. But the life of the seed, the finding of the bread, the recovery of the soul, are as real as the preliminary sacrifice. Hence it is truly said of heaven " in heaven there is no ownership. If any there took upon him to call anything his own, he would straightway be thrust out into hell and become an evil spirit." [1] But it is also said " To him that overcometh I will give a white stone, and in the stone a new name written, which no man knoweth saving he that receiveth it ".[2] What can be more a man's own than this new name which even in eternity remains a secret between God and him? And what shall we take this secrecy to mean? Surely, that each

[1] *Theologia Germanica,* LI.
[2] Rev. ii, 17.

of the redeemed shall forever know and praise some
one aspect of the divine beauty better than any other
creature can. Why else were individuals created, but
that God, loving all infinitely, should love each
differently? And this difference, so far from impairing,
floods with meaning the love of all blessed creatures
for one another, the communion of the saints. If
all experienced God in the same way and returned
Him an identical worship, the song of the Church
triumphant would have no symphony, it would be like
an orchestra in which all the instruments played the
same note. Aristotle has told us that a city is a unity
of unlikes,[1] and St. Paul that a body is a unity of
different members.[2] Heaven is a city, and a Body,
because the blessed remain eternally different: a
society, because each has something to tell all the
others—fresh and ever fresh news of the " My God "
whom each finds in Him whom all praise as " Our
God ". For doubtless the continually successful, yet
never completed, attempt by each soul to com-
municate its unique vision to all others (and that by
means whereof earthly art and philosophy are but
clumsy imitations) is also among the ends for which
the individual was created.

For union exists only between distincts; and,
perhaps, from this point of view, we catch a momentary glimpse of the meaning of all things. Pantheism
is a creed not so much false as hopelessly behind the
times. Once, before creation, it would have been
true to say that everything was God. But God
created: He caused things to be other than Himself

---

[1] *Politics*, II, 2, 4.
[2] 1 Cor. xii, 12–30.

that, being distinct, they might learn to love Him, and achieve union instead of mere sameness. Thus He also cast His bread upon the waters. Even within the creation we might say that inanimate matter, which has no will, is one with God in a sense in which men are not. But it is not God's purpose that we should go back into that old identity (as, perhaps, some Pagan mystics would have us do) but that we should go on to the maximum distinctness there to be re-united with Him in a higher fashion. Even within the Holy One Himself, it is not sufficient that the Word should *be* God, it must also be *with* God. The Father eternally begets the Son and the Holy Ghost proceeds : deity introduces distinction within itself so that the union of reciprocal loves may transcend mere arithmetical unity or self identity.

But the eternal distinctness of each soul—the secret which makes of the union between each soul and God a species in itself—will never abrogate the law that forbids ownership in heaven. As to its fellow-creatures, each soul, we suppose, will be eternally engaged in giving away to all the rest that which it receives. And as to God, we must remember that the soul is but a hollow which God fills. Its union with God is, almost by definition, a continual self-abandonment—an opening, an unveiling, a surrender, of itself. A blessed spirit is a mould ever more and more patient of the bright metal poured into it, a body ever more completely uncovered to the meridian blaze of the spiritual sun. We need not suppose that the necessity for something analogous to self-conquest will ever be ended, or that eternal life will not also be eternal dying. It is in this sense

that, as there may be pleasures in hell (God shield us
from them), there may be something not all unlike
pains in heaven (God grant us soon to taste them).

For in self-giving, if anywhere, we touch a rhythm
not only of all creation but of all being. For the
Eternal Word also gives Himself in sacrifice; and
that not only on Calvary. For when He was crucified
He " did that in the wild weather of His outlying
provinces which He had done at home in glory and
gladness ".[1] From before the foundation of the world
He surrenders begotten Deity back to begetting
Deity in obedience. And as the Son glorifies the
Father, so also the Father glorifies the Son.[2] And,
with submission, as becomes a layman, I think it was
truly said " God loveth not Himself as Himself but as
Goodness; and if there were aught better than God,
He would love that and not Himself ".[3] From the
highest to the lowest, self exists to be abdicated and,
by that abdication, becomes the more truly self, to
be thereupon yet the more abdicated, and so forever.
This is not a heavenly law which we can escape by
remaining earthly, nor an earthly law which we can
escape by being saved. What is outside the system of
self-giving is not earth, nor nature, nor " ordinary
life ", but simply and solely Hell. Yet even Hell
derives from this law such reality as it has. That
fierce imprisonment in the self is but the obverse of the
self-giving which is absolute reality; the negative
shape which the outer darkness takes by surrounding
and defining the shape of the real, or which the real

---

[1] George Macdonald. *Unspoken Sermons : 3rd Series*, pp. 11, 12.
[2] John xvii, 1, 4, 5.
[3] *Theol. Germ.*, XXXII.

imposes on the darkness by having a shape and positive nature of its own.

The golden apple of selfhood, thrown among the false gods, became an apple of discord because they scrambled for it. They did not know the first rule of the holy game, which is that every player must by all means touch the ball and then immediately pass it on. To be found with it in your hands is a fault : to cling to it, death. But when it flies to and fro among the players too swift for eye to follow, and the great master Himself leads the revelry, giving Himself eternally to His creatures in the generation, and back to Himself in the sacrifice, of the Word, then indeed the eternal dance " makes heaven drowsy with the harmony ". All pains and pleasures we have known on earth are early initiations in the movements of that dance : but the dance itself is strictly incomparable with the sufferings of this present time. As we draw nearer to its uncreated rhythm, pain and pleasure sink almost out of sight. There is joy in the dance, but it does not exist for the sake of joy. It does not even exist for the sake of good, or of love. It is Love Himself, and Good Himself, and therefore happy. It does not exist for us, but we for it. The size and emptiness of the universe which frightened us at the outset of this book, should awe us still, for though they may be no more than a subjective bye-product of our three dimensional imagining, yet they symbolise great truth. As our Earth is to all the stars, so doubtless are we men and our concerns to all creation ; as all the stars are to space itself, so are all creatures, all thrones and powers and mightiest of the created gods, to the abyss of the self-existing Being, who is to us Father and Redeemer and indwelling Comforter, but of whom no man nor angel can say nor conceive what He is in and for Himself, or what is the work that he " maketh from the beginning to the end ". For they are all derived and unsubstantial things. Their vision fails them and they cover their eyes from the intolerable light of utter actuality, which was and is and shall be, which never could have been otherwise, which has no opposite.

APPENDIX

(This note on the observed effects of pain has been kindly supplied by R. Havard, M.D., from clinical experience.)

PAIN is a common and definite event which can easily be recognised : but the observation of character or behaviour is less easy, less complete, and less exact, especially in the transient, if intimate, relation of doctor and patient. In spite of this difficulty certain impressions gradually take form in the course of medical practice which are confirmed as experience grows. A short attack of severe physical pain is overwhelming while it lasts. The sufferer is not usually loud in his complaints. He will beg for relief but does not waste his breath on elaborating his troubles. It is unusual for him to lose self-control and to become wild and irrational. It is rare for the severest physical pain to become in this sense unbearable. When short, severe, physical pain passes it leaves no obvious alteration in behaviour. Long-continued pain has more noticeable effects. It is often accepted with little or no complaint and great strength and resignation are developed. Pride is humbled or, at times, results in a determination to conceal suffering. Women with rheumatoid arthritis show a cheerfulness which is so characteristic that it can be compared to the *spes phthisica* of the consumptive : and is perhaps due more to a slight intoxication of the patient by the infection than to an increased strength of character. Some victims of chronic pain deteriorate. They become querulous and exploit their privileged position as invalids to practise domestic tyranny. But the wonder is that the failures are so few and the heroes so many; there is a challenge in physical pain which most can recognise and answer. On the other hand, a long illness, even without pain, exhausts the mind as well as the body. The invalid gives up the struggle and drifts helplessly and plaintively into a self-pitying despair. Even so, some, in a similar physical state, will preserve their serenity and selflessness to the end. To see it is a rare but moving experience.

Mental pain is less dramatic than physical pain, but it is more common and also more hard to bear. The frequent attempt to conceal mental pain increases the burden : it is easier to say " My tooth is aching " than to say " My heart is broken ". Yet if the cause is accepted and faced, the conflict will strengthen and purify the character and in time the pain will usually pass. Sometimes, however, it persists and the effect is devastating; if the cause is not faced or not recognised, it produces the dreary state of the chronic neurotic. But some by heroism overcome even chronic mental pain. They often produce brilliant work and strengthen, harden, and sharpen their characters till they become like tempered steel.

In actual insanity the picture is darker. In the whole realm of medicine there is nothing so terrible to contemplate as a man with chronic melancholia. But most of the insane are not unhappy or, indeed, conscious of their condition. In either case, if they recover, they are surprisingly little changed. Often they remember nothing of their illness.

Pain provides an opportunity for heroism; the opportunity is seized with surprising frequency.

INDEX

Books by C. S. Lewis

The Problem of Pain

The Great Divorce

Mere Christianity

The Screwtape Letters

Screwtape Proposes a Toast

Surprised by Joy

The Four Loves

Reflections on the Psalms

Miracles

Prayer: Letters to Malcolm

Fern-seed and Elephants